RELEASING YOUR NEED TO PLEASE

by

James Butler, BA, BSW, RSW

A Wood Dragon Book

RELEASING YOUR NEED TO PLEASE

Escaping Romantic Relationships with Narcissistic Women

by

James Butler, BA, BSW, RSW

A Wood Dragon Book

Releasing Your Need To Please - *Escaping Romantic*
Relationships with Narcissistic Women

Copyright © 2023 James Butler

Disclaimer: If you have any significant pleasing or narcissistic
tendencies, you may see yourself in this book—at least
to some degree. But rest assured, the content does not
mirror any specific individual. It may seem so—in that
the thought patterns, words, feelings, and behaviors of
both pleasers and narcissists are remarkably consistent.
It is a composite of the hundreds of individuals the
author has worked with over the past two decades.

Inside design by: Christine Lee
Cover design by: Yago Domingues

Published by:
Wood Dragon Books
Box 429, Mossbank, Saskatchewan, Canada, S0H 3G0
http://www.wooddragonbooks.com

ISBN: 978-1-990863-30-1 (Paperback)
ISBN: 978-1-990863-29-5 (eBook)
ISBN: 978-1990863-54-7 (Hardcover)

To contact the author: https://acacounselling.ca

DEDICATION

To my children, April and Colby, who
have taught me so much about courage,
personal responsibility, honesty, trust—and
most importantly—unconditional love.

CONTENTS

DISCLAIMER

If you are looking for a book to help you *fix* your emotionally abusive relationship, this book is not for you. If instead, you are looking for help to *escape* your toxic relationship, this book *is* definitely for you. The reality is, you don't know what you don't know. And in order to be successful during this frightening process, you will require a specific knowledge base, skill set, and airtight plan. *Releasing Your Need to Please* is written for the male partner in an abusive relationship—who just happens to be a pleaser. Ultimately, the book's purpose is to provide a road map *out* of abusive relationships. It is a wake-up call to assist the pleaser to let go of his addictive need to re-engage with his mate—if he is ultimately to save himself. In other words, he must shift his hope from fixing or saving his abusive mate—to fixing and saving himself. This book is written for *men who are ready* to resolve the issue of their own abuse and help them to develop the confidence and self-esteem they will need to escape.

If you happen *to be a woman* looking for help to escape an abusive relationship, the information in this book will most certainly help you as well. Although the cases in this book are specific to male pleasers and female narcissists, the knowledge base and strategies for escape are as applicable to women as they are to men.

If you have any significant pleasing or narcissistic tendencies, you may *see yourself* in this book—at least to some degree. But rest assured, *the content does not mirror any specific individual*. It may seem so—in that the thought patterns, words, feelings, and behaviors of both pleasers and narcissists are remarkably consistent. After more than seventeen years of counselling both women and men who have sought love with narcissistic individuals, I can almost predict what each of them will say and how they might react—even before we have finished our first session together. This is how common and consistent the insecurities, thoughts, words, and belief systems are within pleasers and narcissists.

This book contains several **_holy shit_** moments—in which I say something that might initially strike a nerve in the reader, only for him or her to later realize what I have said was the truth. A client recently told me, "I initially thought you were full of shit. How could you have known me so well? But when I thought about what you told me, you were right about everything you said." These realizations may be true for you as well. Expect them. Remember, they are designed to help you develop self-awareness and self-esteem.

For the past 17 years, I have counselled hundreds of individuals in abusive relationships—or just after implosion—and had the opportunity to help and study (in detail)—the complex psychological and interpersonal dynamics of both the narcissist and those with extreme pleasing tendencies. I speak bluntly for the purpose of **_waking pleasers up_** from their confusing, dangerous, and deceptive slumber—and help them realize there is no "hope" to fix or salvage an abusive relationship. This is not some "there, there" book for "victims" of narcissistic abuse. The word "victim" implies an individual has no choice—as it pertains to the abuse inflicted upon him. Throughout the book, I make the clear distinction that **_partners in abusive relationships are not victims_**. While **_they are certainly victimized by the verbal abuse_** they experience, each have the choice of whether to tolerate and participate in the abuse—or do something productive about it.

The change process of personal growth that I am about to take you through will not be easy—but last I checked, getting beat down on a regular basis is not easy either. In fact, it is debilitatingly painful and humiliating. The development of self-awareness and self-esteem (personal power)—involves confronting your fears and abandonment issues—and ultimately releasing your dependency needs. For such important work to be successful, inspiration, knowledge, and specific strategies are required. *Releasing Your Need to Please* is designed to push you, motivate you, and propel you forward—towards making the only healthy and responsible decision before you—a decision that will bring the resolution to your abuse and teach you the value of liking, trusting, and respecting yourself.

DEFINITIONS

Implosion: The sudden collapse of an abusive relationship that results from the culmination of intensifying abusive cycles between a narcissist and a pleaser.

Narcissist and pleaser: The terms *narcissist* and *pleaser* are consistently used throughout the book to describe the insecure attachment styles of the two individuals within an abusive relationship. These highly toxic, dependent relationships consist of an individual with a narcissistic personality disorder—and an individual with extreme pleasing tendencies.

Partner: The partner refers to a pleaser in a narcissistic relationship.

Regulating emotions: The concept of *regulating emotions* is discussed throughout the book. A pleaser attempts to do the emotional labor for his narcissistic mate, to regulate her emotions with the goal of keeping her stable and happy.

Trauma bond: The connection created by the repetitive cycle of neediness and pleasing between a narcissist and a pleaser.

Introduction

I am not what happened to me. I am what I choose to become.
Carl Jung

Narcissistic relationships are often understood to be gender specific—with a man perpetrating the abuse and a women finding herself on the receiving end. While this is certainly the case in many instances, this book is written to explore the growing phenomenon of women who perpetrate narcissistic abuse against their male partners.

Narcissism is ***not*** a gender specific personality disorder. A narcissistic female (a girlfriend or wife) is a traumatized individual who, at her core, feels empty, lonely, powerless, and needful. Deeply insecure within herself, she takes things personally—feeling self-conscious and competitive in her romantic relationships. Her self-loathing and needfulness are most obvious in her relationship with a love partner.

A narcissistic woman lives only to please and protect her ego. While she acts like she is better and brighter than others, her insecurities are easily triggered. In order to soothe feelings of loneliness, needfulness, and self-loathing, she requires a love partner—even though she has no love to give, or empathy for the feelings of others.

To be clear, narcissistic individuals (both men and women) abound. Narcissism, itself, is a disorder that stems from childhood trauma. And since most of these individuals avoid the light-shedding process of therapy, I find myself working with their partners, all of whom just happen to be *pleasers*. While pleasers are more open to self-reflection than their narcissistic counterparts, helping them accept that pleasing and putting their mate before themselves is never going to fix their abusive relationship—is no easy task.

Becoming aware of their unhealthy attachment style (or trauma bond) and beginning to release their need to please—is not something the pleaser is always interested in doing—until he is *ready*. While pleasers often seek out counselling, the help they are looking for is often not geared towards working on themselves, but instead fixing their abusive relationship. They often come to my office wanting to figure out how they can better communicate with their narcissistic counterpart—as if communication was the primary issue in need of attention. Pleasers can be resistant to acknowledging their narcissistic mate is unwilling to change—and that the toleration and participation of the abuse is extremely damaging to their own mental health.

Each pleaser I work with objects to the irresponsible, controlling, volatile, manipulative, and unstable nature of their narcissistic mate, yet most resist looking at *why* they choose to tolerate such insidious treatment. Some seem resistant to an exploration of what they, *themselves*, can do about their own abuse. For the most part, their sole focus is to get their girlfriend or wife to treat them better—as if that were possible.

Despite feeling exhausted and "trapped," some already know they are in an abusive relationship, yet remain resistant to letting go of their "hope" that the relationship can be salvaged. Rather than focusing on what they must do to free themselves from the chains of their abuse, pleasers come to therapy wanting me to tell them how to improve their communication with their abusive mate. If they can better communicate, pleasers think they can prevent their mate from becoming defensive, unstable, hostile, and manipulative—hoping they will then not have to escape their abusive relationship.

Failing to understand their mate's pathology of narcissism—and the permanence of their abuse—pleasers tend to believe they will eventually get through to their narcissistic mate and, as a result, cling to the hope they can fix their abusive relationship.

I am often informed, "I am not a quitter" or "I don't want to feel like a failure"—as if getting out of an abusive relationship is "quitting" or "failing"—as opposed to letting go and starting to care for oneself. Others refuse to admit to themselves they are in an abusive relationship, even though they have some awareness on a deeper level. They tell themselves, "If I admit I'm in an abusive relationship, then I feel a lot of shame." Self-deception plays a major role in the pleaser's dangerous decision to stay in his abusive relationship.

Pleasers are often more aware of their abuse than they admit to themselves—or anyone else for that matter. They are adept at rationalizing the abusive relationship is better than it is—in order to repress deep trauma and fears of confronting the perceived pain of separation. In addition, they have adapted to the abuse, to the point it has become their "normal."

If pleasers admit the truth to themselves, that they are, in fact, in an abusive relationship—and that the abuse will only accelerate in frequency and intensity—they are then required to do something about it. This would mean getting real with themselves and beginning to work through abandonment and dependency issues (their own dependent chains of pleasing). Instead, pleasers prefer to repress this terror—at the expense of their psychological well-being (loss of identity, autonomy, and feelings of self-worth). Apparently, it is easier to lose themselves and become a "victim," than accept the responsibility for protecting themselves—by no longer engaging with their abusive mate hoping that she will one day change.

Pleasers have some similarities with their narcissistic counterparts. Both were traumatized as children and have not yet recovered. Both have low self-worth that create an extremely high need for external approval. And both are terrified of abandonment, rejection, and being alone.

Lack of self-awareness and self-esteem is the core issue of an abusive relationship.

Pleasers are emotionally repressed individuals who tend to trivialize or normalize early, traumatic experiences—in which they learned perfectionistic behaviors designed to seek parental approval, love, and acceptance. They were not permitted to be themselves as children and internalized feelings something was "flawed" or "wrong" with them.

Just like the narcissist, a pleaser is wounded from childhood trauma and, as a result, remains deeply insecure within himself. He feels no sense of intrinsic value in his romantic relationships and, therefore, prioritizes his mate's needs, wants, and feelings over his own. The pleaser puts himself on the back burner in order to impress and prove himself to his mate—for the sole purpose of "keeping her happy" and avoid further abuse or add rejection.

Being attracted to—and staying with—a narcissistic woman is the result of the pleaser's unresolved childhood trauma. Experiencing old feelings of guilt, shame, worthlessness, failure, and terror of further abuse, pleasers seek to *fix* their abusive relationship—by accommodating the coercive manipulation of their mate.

Clearly, accommodation and submission are maladaptive coping strategies. Sometimes with the best of intentions, pleasers cannot seem to figure out why they have experienced a series of toxic relationships—and why they are now sitting in my office—feeling trapped, stuck, confused, defeated, and exhausted. Many are not ready to ask **why** they often find themselves treated poorly by others, and instead prefer to sweep their fears and insecurities under the carpet—only to focus on how they might somehow stop offending their narcissistic mate.

Having rushed into another romantic relationship (unaware or unwilling to confront their own deep need to please), pleasers find themselves dealing with a highly insecure, controlling, vitriolic, manipulative, and unstable woman. Then, as they always do, they blame themselves for their mate's manipulative, unstable behavior—while, at the same time, hoping she will change once she realizes what she is doing.

For many of these individuals, it appears that no amount of manipulation and unpredictable abuse from their mate—will prompt them to make the critical decision to escape the relationship and break their chains of pleasing. Chronically second-guessing themselves—or feeling sorry for their mate—pleasers struggle with the notion they must learn to stand up for themselves, by finally putting themselves first.

Many pleasers are not interested in learning to stand up for themselves and beginning to put themselves first.

These changes require the regulation of their own feelings. Pleasers are terrified to feel the perceived pain of change, uncertainty, abandonment, loss, fall-out, and letting go. It is this terror that keep pleasers "stuck" or "chained" in their own indecisive, mistrust of themselves.

Over the years, I have heard a litany of rationalizations and excuses for staying:

- "We've built a life together. I don't want to give that all up."
- "I see myself as a committed family man."
- "I don't want to have to start over."
- "I'm staying for the children."
- "I'm hoping things will get better."
- "I don't want to feel like a failure."
- "I'm not a quitter."
- "She had a difficult childhood."
- "I believe I'll be able to get her to see that I'm not trying to offend her."

Other clients are more vulnerable about their feelings, including the fear of backlash should they decide to end their narcissistic relationship:

- "I feel I'm too weak to leave."
- "I've been beat down for so long."
- "I'm terrified about what she will do if I leave."
- "She's already threatened to take the children. I know her. She'll make good on her threats."
- "My children are my life. There's no way I could handle losing them."
- "I'm terrified to be alone."

The idea of making the difficult (yet critical) decision to escape is so terrifying that many would rather lose themselves (their autonomy, sanity, identity, and self-worth) in the abusive relationship, than face the terror (and emotional pain) of separation, abandonment, change, uncertainty, grief, being alone, and a possible custody battle.

> While pleasers justify staying in the relationship, abusive relationships are not sustainable. This is why I have written this book—to give you the knowledge and the skills required to break your chains (that keep you trapped) and escape your abuse.

It is critical that individuals in abusive relationships learn about the pathology of narcissism and begin releasing their own need to please. They need to come to understand **why** pleasers and narcissists always attract—and why they cling to each other in a way that defies logic, reason, or common sense. Pleasers need to learn the psychological consequences of narcissistic abuse. Chronic feelings of confusion, anxiety, self-doubt, defeat, worthlessness, mental anguish, panic attacks, and loss of identity are just a few. Then, they must decide to detach, disengage, and let go of their dangerous relationship—to sever the chains of their mate's control—as well as the chains of their own dependency issues.

The irresponsible and dangerous decision to stay is not without severe psychological consequences. While most innately know this, they hold deep beliefs that they do not deserve to be treated better. Because of low self-worth stemming from childhood trauma, many pleasers require help in order to ready themselves to leave their abusive relationships— and work through the process of confronting and experiencing their own painful emotions. And when they exercise the courage, knowledge, and skills needed—to build trust within themselves—they develop the confidence to finally escape the hell that has become their comfort zone.

> Contrary to popular belief, a pleaser is not a *victim*—
> unless, of course, he chooses to make himself one.

I'm often told by clients that too many therapists take a "there, there" approach to abusive relationships, offering little, if any, real help. And to be fair, not all pleasers are interested, or ready to escape. With this in mind, I will not be discussing (or embracing) the traditional perpetrator-victim approach (in which the narcissist is the "villain" and the partner is the "victim"). This outdated paradigm is not helpful in terms of empowering individuals to make the critical decision to escape.

The term *victim* implies that a partner has no choice. All partners in narcissistic relationships have choices—and they have all had choices from the very beginning of the relationship. Every client I have ever worked with has acknowledged there were red flags in the early stages of their abusive relationship—and many of them feel deep shame for having made the decision to stay.

Viewing yourself to be a victim in a narcissistic relationship is about the worst thing you can do—which is why this book does not endorse a "there, there" approach for partners in abusive relationships, nor does it subscribe to a "victim" mentality. After seventeen years of counselling in private practice, I am confident in saying that all partners in abusive relationships are pleasers. Although they are most certainly **victimized** by verbal abuse, they all have the choice to leave. In other words, they can only be victims so long as they stay in the abusive relationship.

**This is why I have written this book, and why its timing is crucial.
It is written for men who are ready to do something about their
abuse—and to stand up for themselves and their children.**

The book is designed to help men understand the dangerous reality of abusive relationships with narcissistic women—and to understand the characteristics and psychological dynamics both the pleaser and narcissist bring to the toxic relationship. Its purpose is to offer information about how to get out of unfixable, unsustainable, dangerous relationships.

Throughout the book, my message is clear. You can choose to see yourself as a victim without choice (or power), or you can choose to empower yourself, escape, and be happy. *The choice is yours. So are the consequences.* It is time men understood the real danger of staying in abusive relationships with narcissistic women—both for themselves—and for their children. They need to know why separation is the only reasonable and healthy path forward.

By learning about the dependency issues inherent in narcissism and pleasing, men can choose to embark on the rewarding process of personal growth (a major theme of this book). Once engaged in the process of self-improvement, they then put themselves in the optimal position of reclaiming their personal power. In order to grow as an individual (as opposed to the alternative of decay), it is imperative to accept that abusive relationships cannot be repaired, salvaged, or fixed. In reality, this is good news because you can now reframe your abusive relationship into a positive opportunity for healing and personal growth.

The narcissist can ultimately be a catalyst for personal growth by essentially forcing you to choose your own wants, needs, and feelings over that of your mate's—and to ultimately let go of your need for her approval and love.

By learning to like, trust, and respect yourself (as opposed to regulating the emotions and behavior of your narcissistic mate at the expense of your own), you can develop the inner strength to escape. This book will teach you how to put yourself first—and to stand up for yourself and your children. The process begins with getting honest with yourself— and ultimately accepting you have no other reasonable choice but to get ready to escape the chains of your abusive relationship. Honesty with self is critical to making this decision.

This book is written for the pleaser. Its true purpose is to teach him to break the chains of his abusive relationship— before his mate implodes and does this for him.

As a therapist, I am keenly aware of the guilt, shame, hurt, confusion, and humiliation that result from the manipulative battering of a narcissist. I am also attuned to how the pleaser tolerates his own battering—by convincing himself he can "fix" the problem of his own abuse—by morphing himself into whoever his mate needs him to be.

Pleasers need to develop self-esteem—by learning to like, trust, and respect themselves. This is accomplished by regulating their own feelings, including their anxiety regarding conflict, disapproval, rejection and abuse—by releasing their dependency and abandonment issues—and the various chains that keep them "stuck" in their abusive relationship. They must accept they are powerless to help, fix, or "save" their narcissistic mate.

> The pleaser must accept he is powerless to change or fix anyone other than himself. This book will help the reader gradually release himself from his need and desire for his mate's approval, acceptance, and love—a need and desire he will never fulfill.

Releasing your chains—the need to please—involves the process of differentiation, in which you begin to define yourself, set and hold boundaries, regulate your emotions, and manage the anxiety that comes from conflict, abuse, and separation. By learning the skills of disengagement and detachment—and recognizing covert anger and manipulation—you will develop *trust* in yourself, a crucial component of self-esteem.

As you begin trusting yourself, your need for approval is ultimately released—and the chains of approval-seeking are severed. This need is replaced by the awareness that you must stand up for yourself—and plan your escape.

The information and concepts presented in this book stem from my seventeen years of day-to-day clinical practice with clients who have struggled in hostile, dependent relationships—in which they have actively avoided conflict, repressed their emotions, and continued to please their hostile mates. As as they have engaged in these self-sabotaging behaviors, they unwittingly gave their identity, autonomy, freedom, and personal power away. Many actively avoided the process of personal growth—by excusing, rationalizing, and trivializing their own abuse—and by deceiving themselves that they have the power to fix their toxic mate.

While narcissism and pleasing are equally applicable to both sexes, this book is written for men who are pleasers, who feel "trapped" or "chained" inside an abusive relationship. It is my sincere hope that this book empowers men to take their mental health (and that of their children's) more seriously than they currently do. By getting started on this courageous and inspiring journey, partners must first acknowledge they *are* being abused and make the critical decision to escape. The days of putting their mate's wants, needs, and feelings before their own—in an effort to earn love, and prove themselves—must finally come to an end.

When men learn about the dangerous pathology of narcissism and their own need to please—and then practice the confidence-building strategies outlined in this book—they will see what is going on in the mind of their narcissistic girlfriend or wife. With this invaluable insight, they will realize just how damaged their lover is and how the abusive relationship will only get worse over time—no matter how hard they keep trying—or how much hope they keep clinging to.

Many of the courageous clients I have worked with over the years who have already developed the awareness, skills, and strength to break the chains of their abusive relationships, have gone on to create self-esteem, happiness, and satisfying romantic relationships. Each eventually came to terms with the fact that they could not change their narcissistic mate—and accepted that the only person they could change was themselves. They realized they deserved more than the insidious treatment they were receiving. Once these clients became aware they had the power to change themselves, they realized they were not victims—and that they had choices all along, however terrifying or unwanted those choices seemed to be at the time.

Should you reframe your narcissist mate to be a catalyst for your personal growth, ultimately forcing you out of your powerless dependency of pleasing and onto the path of self-awareness and increased self-esteem, you can use your relationship as a platform—to learn to stand up for yourself—and break the chains of your own abuse. As you break your chains of pleasing, you learn to protect and care for yourself—by putting yourself and your children first.

When my clients have realigned their perceptions from seeing themselves as "failures" for "giving up" and leaving an abusive relationship—to perceiving themselves as successful individuals who have learned to trust themselves—they become motivated to renew their determination to leave. As each begin this process, they embark upon the remarkable journey of personal growth and learn that healthy romantic love is never going to happen—until, or unless, they learn to like, trust, and respect themselves.

You can learn how to break your chains of pleasing—as well as escape the chains of your mate's control. This book is about to take you on a courageous, empowering, and rewarding journey. Are you *ready?*

1

The Narcissist and the Pleaser: The Early Dynamics of a Psychologically Abusive Relationship

If you are reading this book, you are likely feeling beat-down, defeated, and stuck in a narcissistic relationship. Perhaps you have already escaped, only to find yourself in the post-separation fall-out phase of your relationship, fighting for shared custody of your children, and desperately trying to get your mate to stop her vitriolic campaign of revenge. Whatever your current predicament, it is imperative you understand the psychological dynamics of a narcissistic relationship— if you are to make the decision to escape, minimize the fall-out, and insulate yourself from ongoing abuse after separation.

Let's begin by looking at the two most prevalent, underlying dynamics in any psychologically abusive relationship: *Neediness* and *Pleasing*. Both stem from the insecure attachment styles of the narcissist and pleaser, and both are caused by childhood trauma, low self-esteem, and dependency issues.

An abusive relationship centers around the narcissist's neediness and the pleaser's need for approval. Early in the relationship, the pleaser is interested in locking down his new girlfriend, and enjoys the fact she wants to spend so much time together. It means she is interested—and desires a romantic relationship with him. The pleaser eventually becomes aware of his mate's needful nature and soon becomes overwhelmed—yet lacks the self-awareness to know what he is dealing with. His mate's frequent need for attention, validation, emotional support, and care soon take precedence over his own wants and needs. Beginning to notice his mate's needful personality, he hopes that the situation is only temporary—and that his mate will soon tire of requiring so much attention and care.

> Terrified of conflict and potential rejection, the pleaser does not communicate his feelings about his mate's neediness, even though he may be running out of steam. Instead, he believes he can satisfy his mate and hopes this will only be a phase.

Underneath these behavioral dynamics, the pleaser does not feel deserving of his new love interest. His mate is just what he has been looking for. The pleaser's attraction is often based solely on the physical. But soon he realizes his attraction comes at quite the cost—as she is frequently pressuring him to get together more than he desires. The fact that she is interested soon turns from a good thing to requiring a break from her neediness.

From the outset, the narcissist requires significant attention and care to keep her happy and satisfied. She loves to hear herself talk, but shows little interest in listening to what her partner has to say. She often likes to brag about herself and complain about others. Soon the pleaser observes a discrepancy between who his narcissistic mate claims to be—and who she really is. While she claims to be virtuous, kind, and healthy, she is needy and controlling.

Whatever topic she wants to discuss *will* be the topic at hand, as the narcissist demands the attention and validation of her partner. The pleaser soon sees his mate's tendency towards self-absorption, but believes it will stop once she feels more secure in the relationship. He remains hopeful that the one-directional relationship will become more of a partnership over time.

Most partners are initially surprised when they attempt to participate, interject, or offer a different opinion in the one-way conversations that have come to define the relationship. Their mate's reactions are swift:

- "You're interrupting me."
- "You aren't letting me finish."
- "You always have to have the last word."

Yet the partner did not interrupt. Did let her finish. And did not try to have the last word. Soon he becomes confused—because he does not recognize the manipulative words of his mate. The partner views her reactions to be "misunderstandings" and, as a result, begins to second guess himself:

- "Maybe it is me needing the last word and I just don't see it."
- "Maybe I am interrupting and just don't think I am."

The partner is now dealing with subtle manipulation but cannot recognize it. Instead, he falsely sees his mate's sharp reactions to be "misunderstandings."

As the relationship progresses, the partner begins to increasingly doubt himself. He also becomes exhausted—attempting to meet the many needs of his narcissistic mate—and finds himself wanting to have more time away from the relationship. He recognizes his new girlfriend wants to get together more than he would like to, but does not speak his truth or dare set a firm boundary. When he does attempt to tell his mate he needs a little time to himself, he finds himself manipulated to be "selfish" or "uncaring," or both.

- "I don't understand why you wouldn't want to be with me?"

- "I don't say 'no' to you."
- "I don't understand how you can be so uncaring."
- "Why would you not want to be with me?"
- "Maybe you aren't the person I should be with."

The moment the narcissist does not get her way, she manipulates her mate to feel he has said something wrong or offensive—when, in fact, he has not. For example, should he be visiting at his mate's place—and communicate he needs to go home because of an early morning at work, the partner may be pressured to ignore his wants and needs—in favor of his mate's.

- "If you stay until midnight, you'll still get seven hours sleep."
- "You can sleep tomorrow after work."
- "You don't seem to want to spend as much time with me anymore."

Being a pleaser, the partner is terrified to speak his truth or confront his mate about her neediness and the pressure she often puts on him to be with her. At his core, he feels he does not deserve her—and may very well lose her if he no longer meets her needs and keeps her happy. The process of abandoning himself has begun. The pleaser is frequently met with opposition when he has wants and needs of his own. Should he attempt to explain and justify his need to be elsewhere, he is manipulated to be "selfish," "uncaring," or "neglectful."

> **As the narcissist begins to exert control, the pleaser submits—because he is terrified of losing her.**

Essentially, the partner is made to feel guilty—or otherwise manipulated to be "failing" as an adequate love partner. As a pleaser, he feels significant anxiety when he is met with disapproval or guilt-inducing power plays. He then begins to do what all pleasers do in romantic relationships—he sets about accommodating the needs of his new girlfriend—at the expense of himself.

This is how narcissistic relationships begin, strengthen, and intensify. The narcissist uses coercive manipulation to exert control and the pleaser keeps trying to accommodate his mate's extensive well of need.

Should you see yourself in this dynamic, and recognize your mate's control and manipulation has increased over time—along with your need to "keep her happy" and meet her endless list of expectations, you are in a narcissistic relationship. It is likely you have ignored these signs and signals, in favor of rationalizing that things will eventually get better.

You have been agreeable and accommodating to the point of exhaustion, yet may not recognize the coercive manipulation— or have the words to describe what you are experiencing.

This is where I come in. Unless you are a therapist, you would have falsely perceived your mate's manipulation to be "misunderstandings." Hence, you internalized many of her judgments and accusations about you along the way—that *it is you* who is frequently intending, saying, or doing something "wrong," "offensive," or "malicious."

Pleasing—through accommodation, submission, or compromising yourself—is how pleasers avoid the risk of disapproval, conflict, potential rejection, and coercive manipulation.

Without having the emotional awareness or a sound knowledge base of narcissism and pleasing, you were likely confused about what was happening in your budding relationship—and how your autonomy and character were literally under attack. You were not aware of what was happening in your new romantic relationship and how your personal power was being stolen via manipulative power plays.

I have worked with many pleasers over the years who were not conscious of their childhood trauma. Some had parents that held unrealistic expectations and regularly guilted or blamed them. Hence, these children internalized the blame from their parents and came to believe something was fundamentally wrong with them. Now, in their romantic relationships, these same individuals avoid conflict and repress their emotions—to protect themselves from the fear of conflict, abuse, and the risk of potential rejection. Just like it was when they were a child with their self-absorbed parents, discussing their feelings and needs with their self-absorbed mate is like hitting a brick wall.

Like narcissism, pleasing is an insecure attachment style—resulting from childhood trauma caused by maladaptive parenting. As children, these individuals were forced to earn the love and approval of their parents, by sacrificing their own feelings, wants, and needs. They had to become whoever their parents needed them to be. Under such oppressive conditions (with emotionally unavailable parents), pleasers did not learn to validate their own emotions and, as a result, could not learn to like, respect, and trust themselves later in their romantic relationships.

Pleasers do not believe they add value to a romantic relationship, other than what they can do for their mate. In order to compensate for a perceived lack of self-worth, they go to great lengths to earn, prove, and win the love of their narcissistic mate—at the expense of themselves.

Under these circumstances, both the pleaser and narcissist form a trauma bond—as both repeat the cycle of neediness and pleasing over and over again. The trauma bond intensifies over time as the narcissist continues to manipulate and the pleaser continues to accommodate. The coercive manipulation actually fuels the partner's inherent need to seek the approval, validation, and love from his narcissistic mate—through pleasing.

By repressing his own emotions and needs, the pleaser seeks to win his mate's love and approval—and avoid potential rejection or manipulation. In this capacity, the pleaser plays an active role in the formation of the trauma bond.

Because of low self-esteem, the pleaser frequently remains in a state of anxiety within his romantic relationship, fearing that one wrong move could result in abandonment—and back to a life of barren solitude. Hence, he remains vigilant to mitigate these risks—by impressing, worshiping, doing, caring, and morphing himself into whoever his narcissistic mate needs him to be.

Perhaps you see yourself in this dynamic, but rationalized you would eventually get your mate to see how poorly she was treating you—and eventually get her to trust you (even though she so rarely seemed to believe your explanations). Unaware of why she did not trust you, or why she seemed to always make it about her, you hoped you would eventually be able to prove yourself, gain her trust, and thereby fix the relationship.

You would not have known that the narcissist does not trust herself (her perceptions, feelings, and decisions)—and that she projects her unconscious mistrust of self onto you. Hence, she has always falsely perceived you to be untrustworthy, even though you did nothing to warrant this mistrust.

Like a petulant child, each time your mate did not get her way, she accused you of being "unreliable," "uncaring," or "untrustworthy." Not able to recognize the manipulation in the early stages of the relationship, your mate's accusations created self-doubt—and you began to second-guess yourself. The manipulation created an alternate reality—in which your own perceptions conflicted with hers—as to who was causing the conflict in the relationship. However, as a pleaser, you would not have recognized the needfulness and coercive manipulation you were experiencing to be a permanent characteristic of your new girlfriend.

Instead, you went about pleasing (explaining, proving, justifying, and submitting yourself), even though you might have known you did nothing wrong. But, you needed her to stop being upset with you. Hence, you did whatever it took to regain her approval—giving another piece of yourself away each time you accommodated her neediness.

Like the narcissist, the pleaser, too, does not trust himself (his own perceptions, feelings, and decisions). He often projects his unconscious mistrust of self onto the narcissist, but in a different way. He believes his mate is actually credible, honest, reasonable, and trustworthy (for the most part)—even though she has been manipulating him from the get go. He is unaware of his deep mistrust of himself, just as his girlfriend is unaware of hers. Hence, he thinks he can eventually get her to trust him (via pleasing)—and see that he is not trying to offend her.

Having rarely received validation from his parents, the pleaser did not learn to trust his own perceptions, feelings, and decisions growing up. Since his emotional needs were rarely met, he did not learn that his feelings, wants, and needs mattered. In order to emotionally survive, he had to please and often remain invisible.

Because of past trauma, the pleaser does not have the confidence to confront his narcissistic mate. He does not trust his own perceptions and feelings—as to who is creating the conflict in the relationship. In fact, he automatically blames himself when he is met with disapproval, rejection, or manipulation. Not believing he deserves his new girlfriend—he lives in fear of losing her—and remains careful not to screw things up. Hence, the pleaser absorbs his mate's words and represses his emotions—even if he might know he did nothing wrong. Because he fears abandonment, the pleaser does what he has always done—and ignores his own wants and needs to keep his mate happy. For the pleaser (who has no subjective sense of value in a romantic relationship), seeking approval and submitting has always felt like the rational thing to do, even though there is nothing rational about it.

The pleaser believes pleasing and personal compromise (submission) will eventually stop the abuse. He falsely perceives that morphing himself into whoever his mate needs him to be is "giving," when it is not. It is, in fact, his own manipulation (through accommodation) and his own attempt to gain his mate's approval and love. Hence, the pleaser begins the abusive relationship on a false premise—by becoming whoever his mate wants him to be—to make her happy.

> To receive scraps of love and validation, the pleaser is behaving the same way (in his romantic relationship) as he did with his parents. He is replaying childhood trauma in his romantic relationship.

The pleaser attempts to obtain the love he craves—by earning, impressing, pleasing, and winning his mate over. If he can prove his worth—that he is a reliable partner who is willing to do anything for his mate—he believes she will one day trust him and stop her control, judgment, criticism, and neediness. The pleaser is not initially aware his mate is coercing him—via manipulation—to agree with everything she thinks, says, or does.

> Mistrust of self is one of the core insecurities in both the narcissist and pleaser. Each project their mistrust of self onto the other. The pleaser believes he can get his mate to trust him—by morphing himself into whoever she needs him to be—while the narcissist believes her mate can only be trusted if he agrees with everything she says, wants, and does.

The narcissist feels jealous, angry, and betrayed when her mate is wanting to have his own autonomy—whether it be to hang out with friends or spend a quiet night by himself. She becomes frightened and offended when she senses he wants to spend some time away from her—feeling as if she is being rejected when he does not want to spend all of his spare time with her.

Because of her insecurities and neediness, the narcissist wants her partner all to herself—all of the time. She uses coercive manipulation to accomplish this goal—to make her partner feel bad for not wanting to spend more time with her. The manipulation works so effectively because of the pleaser's childhood trauma. Having received significant blame, manipulation, and rejection as a child, he is now vulnerable to the coercive power plays as an adult.

As a child, the pleaser began to blame himself and lose confidence in himself—as he internalized his parents' coercive manipulation. In like fashion, his narcissistic mate was also at the mercy of emotionally unavailable and maladaptive parenting. Like her partner, she internalized the abuse. Hence, she grew up feeling worthless and flawed. Both were traumatized as children and each feel just as they did when they were young, believing that they must be perfect to feel deserving of love.

The narcissist believes she is always right—and requires validation in the form of agreement, while the pleaser must also get validation—but does so by morphing and submitting himself (even when he does not actually agree).

Within this dynamic of worthlessness and perfectionism, both the pleaser and narcissist are playing out childhood trauma within their romantic relationship.

Both have insecure attachment styles—that result in a desperate need for external validation from the partner. Disapproval, disagreement, disappointment, anger, and rejection from the other spark severe interpersonal anxiety in which neither are able to soothe on their own. Each are dependent on the other's approval—to regulate their own interpersonal anxiety. Within their insecure attachment (trauma bond), dependency grows quickly. Each are trying to get more love and validation from the other. It is only their methods of control and manipulation that differ.

Soon the pleaser becomes consumed with anxiety, exhaustion, confusion, shock, humiliation, self-doubt, dread, and feelings of worthlessness. Even so, he is now attached to his narcissistic mate. The physical aspect of the relationship plays a significant part in the strengthening of the trauma bond. Because of abandonment issues, the thought of ending the relationship produces terror and emotional pain. Hence, separation is not something the pleaser is willing to contemplate. Instead, he rationalizes he will eventually be able to prove his love to his narcissistic mate—and when this happens, both will eventually relax into the relationship.

Even as he is treated poorly—and adapting to increasing levels of control—pleasing is all he knows. The pleaser grew up in similar power plays as a child—and emotionally survived by pleasing his parents. Hence, he believes he can eventually make his narcissistic mate happy— by meeting her extensive needs and expectations.

Unfortunately, the pleaser eventually recognizes that once one expectation is met, another is soon to follow. He begins to recognize the self-absorption of his mate, yet willingly participates in the trauma bond—to avoid the risk of abandonment. Eventually, the pleaser attempts to discuss his feelings and needs—out of desperation—only to find himself on the receiving end of more manipulation:

- "I am allowed to have expectations of you."
- "Why don't you want to spend time with me?"
- "I feel you're being selfish and don't want to spend time with me anymore."
- "I am not sure this relationship is going to work."

Herein, the narcissist denies wrong doing—yet her words do not match her behavior. Her double messages create self-doubt and confusion—

of which the pleaser continues to internalize. His mate's denials are manipulative—in that they send the message that something is wrong with him for having concerns with her behavior—as if his feelings are not valid.

Unable to interpret the double messages, the pleaser assumes his mate must be telling the truth—and wracks his brain to figure out *why* his perceptions and feelings are rarely heard or accepted. Yet he holds to the notion he can solve these "misunderstandings" by figuring out why these problems continue to occur.

The pleaser does not recognize the *manipulation* for what it is, nor is he aware of his deep need to please. He does not know what he does not know and, as a result, convinces himself that the only reasonable solution is to try a little harder and do a little more—to satisfy his mate. He hopes he can eventually pull off this impossible task, even as he begins to increasingly doubt himself and becomes overwhelmed by his mate's manipulation. The pleaser does not dare confront the coercive manipulation he is experiencing (if he even sees it at all). Instead, he chooses to tolerate the manipulation and "take it like a man"—believing he will one day be able to prove his love and get through to his narcissistic mate.

After months of tolerating increasing control and manipulation, the pleaser rationalizes it is better to stay—and that things will eventually get better.

Pleasers eventually come to know how excruciatingly painful, humiliating, and debilitating life on the receiving end of abuse is. They often contemplate the idea of leaving, knowing this would probably be the right thing to do yet, due to internal anxiety, they rationalize they can eventually fix the relationship—by submitting and compromising themselves. Even though they may acknowledge what the abuse is doing to them, they stay to avoid the perceived pain of letting go and facing the fall-out.

For these reasons, it is critically important that pleasers accept the following facts about an abusive relationship:

- In a psychologically abusive relationship, the narcissist will continue to pick you apart and find faults where there are none.
- Narcissistic relationships cannot be worked on, salvaged, or fixed—ever.
- There is no "better" way of talking to a narcissist to gain mutual understanding or approval.
- Narcissists have no interest in conflict repair.
- Narcissists only care about winning.
- Narcissistic behavior intensifies the longer the abuse is tolerated.
- Narcissistic relationships are not a villain—victim dynamic.
- Partners have choices. They just do not like the choices they have. They willfully keep making the same, insecure, irrational, dependent choice to remain inside the abusive relationship, hoping it will one day get better.
- In narcissistic relationships, a partner is often portrayed as being trapped against his or her will. This is false.
- Partners attempt to "make" their narcissistic girlfriend or wife treat them better by earning love and proving themselves.
- Partners repeatedly accommodate the manipulation and sell themselves short by compromising themselves—as opposed to disengaging and soothing their interpersonal anxiety in constructive ways.

The above facts are designed to educate men about the reality of their abusive relationship.

All partners have choices. No one is trapped, stuck, or chained in an abusive relationship. They can choose to be a victim, or they can choose to escape and be free. The latter requires knowledge, trust, courage, and dedication to reality.

In many cases, narcissistic women end up being the catalyst for separation. In some inevitable implosion, the police are called—and outrageous accusations are made against the pleaser. Even then, when some are sitting in a jail cell for a couple of days, many still wonder if their mate might take them back after the incident blows over. It is often immediately after implosion when I first meet abused men. They come into my office and describe how they have been criminally charged—and now have to defend themselves from said charges as well as fight to obtain shared custody of their children.

Even when false charges are made, they have been kicked out of their own homes, and children are withheld, abused men still sometimes wish to go back to the "comfort" of what they know. Even though many know how bad their relationship is (on a cognitive level), some would rather remain in the powerless, known comfort of hell—than face an unknown future and the perceived pain of letting go. The hell they know is preferable to the unknown pain they fear. They simply do not believe they deserve better, nor do they believe they are strong enough to make it out.

I am often told:
- "I don't want to have to leave."
- "I still love her."
- "I'm not sure I'm strong enough."
- "I don't want to quit."
- "I feel like a failure."
- "I hope she takes me back."

Do not make the mistake of trivializing the squashing nature of your mate's control and manipulation—or think the abuse has some end date inside the toxic relationship. Your mind is under attack. Do not make the mistake of thinking you can "ride it out" without internalizing the lies against you. Do not think that your capacity to cope with your abuse is not severely compromised over time.

Narcissistic abuse weakens your resilience. But the skills I am about to teach will strengthen and renew your determination to escape.

By no longer giving credibility to the words, perceptions, and feelings of your narcissistic mate, you will begin to let go of your need for her approval—and recognize it is not you causing your own abuse.

Stop blaming yourself for your own abuse. Nothing you say or do is going to stop it. Your mate's manipulative words have the effect of making you believe you are somehow provoking her. Her reactions cause you to blame yourself—and to believe you have somehow intended, said, or did something wrong.

Instead of disengaging and soothing your interpersonal terror, you immediately set about seeking your mate's approval—by apologizing, explaining, proving, submitting, and accepting responsibility for your own abuse. Pleasing in these maladaptive ways only leads to further internalization of the abuse.

By the time pleasers come to see me, I hear the following statements:
- "Maybe it is me."
- "I feel like I'm going crazy."
- "I'm really confused."
- "I cannot figure out if I'm being emotionally abused, or if I'm the one who's abusive."
- "Logically I know I'm not, but emotionally I doubt myself."
- "She always says it is me."
- "I'm often second-guessing myself."
- "I cannot be sure of what's real and what's not anymore."
- "I do get angry, so maybe it *is* me."

Around and around these individuals go—caught in the cycle of abuse, confusion, second-guessing, pleasing, and personal compromise—

which ultimately culminates in exhaustion, emotional anguish, panic-attacks, feelings of worthlessness and defeat.

Often, when I meet these individuals, many pleasers attempt to convince me that they can somehow work things out with their narcissistic mate. They are more than willing to accept responsibility for their mate's abuse—if that means fixing the relationship so they do not have to leave. If they continue to accept responsibility for crap that is **not** theirs to accept, they can avoid the responsibility of soothing their own feelings and confronting their pain of leaving.

> "If it *is all me*, then I can fix my abusive relationship—by trying even harder and accepting even more of the blame."

And there you have it. This is the basic anatomy of the narcissistic relationship, how the trauma bond is formed, and **why** pleasers stay. The partner gives his personal power away by caving, tolerating, rationalizing, and excusing his mate's abusive behavior—all in the hope he can eventually "make her happy" in the end. This is the pleaser's control—and his attempt to get his mate to treat him better—so he can avoid regulating and soothing his own emotions resulting from conflict, abuse, and rejection.

The narcissistic relationship is nothing short of the pursuit for external power over another. Both individuals need to control the other—to feel better about themselves. Each needs the other's love in order to feel secure within themself, which explains why each refuse to let go of the dependent relationship. Both trade their souls for some illusion of what things could be—while blindly refusing to work on themselves and develop self-esteem. The relationship provides an illusion of security and inner value—only so long as each are validated by the other.

If you see yourself in this chapter, and you have been choosing to stay because of your interpersonal terror and lack of self-worth, you will want to read on.

You will ultimately be forced to choose between your two biggest fears:
  (1) Leave—and face the fear of separation, change, grief, letting go, and unknown pain.
  (2) Stay—and continue to lose yourself in a series of manipulative power plays that have nothing to do with love, romance, and respect.

You are never stuck, trapped, or chained in an abusive relationship. You are stuck only in fear, doubt, and low self-esteem.

It is my hope that you apply the knowledge and techniques in this book—and choose to inspire yourself with a renewed determination in yourself—by taking your power back and accepting the only person you can change is you. I hope I have set the stage for what is sure to be a thought provoking, empowering, inward journey—towards escaping your abusive relationship and developing authentic power. Your abusive relationship is certainly not worth your sanity, identity, autonomy, freedom, time, and self-worth. You deserve to be treated a hell of a lot better than you currently are!

2

Bending Over Backwards: A Flight from Freedom

The previous chapter concluded with the two choices you have before you:

(1) Stay in your abusive relationship, hope things eventually work out, and then be shocked when your narcissistic mate implodes

(2) Put your hope in yourself, develop self-confidence, and break the chains of your abusive relationship.

The choice is yours. You have options. You are not "stuck" in an abusive relationship. This type of thinking locks you into a victim mindset. Once you accept that you are not doing yourself (or your children) any favors by remaining in a toxic relationship, you can begin to get real with yourself—by confronting your fears and trusting you are strong enough to make it out. Change is often terrifying. It involves facing the unknown. Escaping an abusive relationship is certainly no exception—but what other reasonable decision do you have?

After seventeen years of working with individuals and couples in hostile-dependent relationships, it is shocking to observe how many individuals distract themselves—by focusing all of their attention on fixing or changing their mate so they do not have to do the work of changing themselves.

Many individuals have been traumatized as children and lack the self-awareness and self-esteem to create a successful romantic relationship. For many, tolerating psychological battering is what they believe they deserve. Instead of making the hard, painful, and reasonable decision to step out of their comfort zone, they choose to remain inside the insanity of abuse, hoping to avoid the difficult process of detachment, healing, and personal growth.

By remaining in a powerless state of dependency, partners trade their mental health and self-esteem for some illusion of security and a few scraps of love that their romantic relationship provides. While many see themselves to be victims in their abusive relationships, clearly they are not. These individuals (pleasers) have made many choices throughout the course of their relationship—that have resulted in them feeling stuck. They have allowed their personal power to be stolen through coercive manipulation—while at the same time, they have given their power away through accommodation and personal compromise. Pleasers do this by making their narcissistic mate responsible for the regulation of their interpersonal anxiety—each time they are met with disapproval, rejection, conflict, guilt-inducing comments, and other forms of abuse.

All individuals are ultimately responsible for the regulation and soothing of their own emotions. Unfortunately, neither the narcissist nor the pleaser has developed the self-esteem to do this difficult emotional work on their own. Instead, each desperately seeks the attention, acceptance, and love from the other, hoping they can get love without ever having to learn to like, trust, respect, or care for themselves.

Self-esteem, love, and happiness must come from within—by healing trauma, working on yourself, and committing to the process of personal growth. Unfortunately, the pleaser and narcissist have not yet done the difficult work of self-improvement. Hence, they quickly form a trauma bond—as they soak up the admiration and love from the other.

Trauma bonds are insecure attachments that intensify into dependency needs—often resulting from the physical aspect of the relationship—and cyclical patterns of control and manipulation.

In an abusive relationship, both the pleaser and narcissist initially present themselves to be kind, well-adjusted, and reasonable people—that would make ideal love partners. Both present a false image of who they are—and attempt to sell themselves as superior (or healthy) individuals that would make exceptional love partners. But behind this pretense, both remain deeply insecure within their romantic relationship. Fears of inadequacy and unlovability permeate their being. Hence, when they meet, each quickly become dependent on the other for acceptance, care, and approval—hoping the other will provide the love that will ultimately make them feel better about themselves.

As described in Chapter 1, the narcissist's neediness soon becomes apparent, but the pleaser hopes his mate's exhausting expectations will be short-lived. Hence, he willingly takes on the job of caring for his mate, making her happy—and supporting her through increasingly apparent depressive episodes. Soon, the narcissist feels comfortable with the arrangement of being so well-taken care of—and comes to expect this amazing treatment.

Even when the pleaser recognizes his mate's neediness, coupled with her depressive episodes, he sweeps these red flags under the carpet. He is not aware of his partner's narcissistic personality disorder and, as a result, remains blind to what he is getting himself into. He is not aware of his girlfriend's childhood trauma—or how she feels "ripped off" and betrayed by her parents—who failed to meet her emotional needs. She holds them responsible for her feelings of hatred towards herself—and believes that there is nothing she could do to feel better about herself. Feeling victimized from a miserable childhood, the narcissist believes she would feel more confident and lovable if only she had been treated better by her parents.

> **Because of her victim mindset, the narcissist believes her salvation lies in the hands of a love parter—if only she can get him to take care of all of her needs.**

Insecure and invulnerable, the narcissist feels entitled because of how poorly she was treated as a child—and now wears her trauma as a badge of honor. She expects to be treated like royalty for what she has gone through—and believes most others have had it much easier than her. Living in a victim mentality and feeling deeply inadequate, the narcissist sees nothing wrong with rushing into the relationship—and wanting to spend every moment together.

When her partner is not near, she feels empty, lonely, and resentful that he is not choosing to be with her. She obsesses about wanting to be with him and feels rejected and jealous that he would choose to spend time with family or friends—instead of choosing to be with her.

As a child, the narcissist was squashed under the oppressive forces of her parents' control. Rarely seen, heard, acknowledged, or validated, she was forced to emotionally shut down to survive her abusive childhood. Hence, she remains "frozen" and invulnerable. In other words, all emotions are deeply repressed. This explains why the narcissist cannot tolerate the pain of self-reproach or confrontation of any kind—without feeling attacked.

Living in her fragile emotional state, the narcissist cannot tolerate painful emotions. Difference in others—of any kind—are falsely perceived to be "stupid," "offensive," or "rejecting." When you are simply expressing your own individuality and autonomy, your narcissistic mate does not believe you have the right to be yourself—to have your own opinions, values, beliefs, and ways of looking at the world—just as her parents did not believe she had the right to have her own feelings, wants, decisions, opinions, and beliefs.

As a child, the narcissist was punished or rejected simply for being herself. Her parents falsely perceived individual autonomy and differences to be bad.

Your narcissistic mate internalized the control and manipulation of her parents—and now hates herself—just as her abusive parents hated themselves. She now projects feelings of self-loathing and hatred of her parents onto you—by judging or demeaning you whenever you exercise your right to your own individuality. Simply for being yourself, your differences ignite mistrust in your mate. She absolutely requires your approval, agreement, and validation—in order to trust she is "right" about her perceptions. Hence, she attacks to get your agreement, so she can soothe her interpersonal anxiety.

For his part, the pleaser is careful not to speak his truth—because of his own childhood trauma. He, too, was abused and rejected by emotionally unavailable parents—whenever he attempted to have a voice or express his own emotions. Because he was forced to shut his emotions down, the pleaser also developed a strong need for approval. Hence, confronting his narcissistic mate involves too much risk of provoking anger, abandonment, or abuse—just as it did when he attempted to express his feelings as a child.

Opening up about why he is feeling exhausted—or needing more time to himself—creates the risk of abandonment. Hence, he keeps his feelings to himself to avoid the risk of conflict, abuse, or rejection. The pleaser mistrusts his own perceptions and emotions—and believes his mate must somehow be right about her perceptions.

Neither the narcissist nor the pleaser trust themselves. Hence, the narcissist projects the maladaptive treatment of her parents (as well as her own insecurities and faults) onto the pleaser—while he internalizes her projections to be his own and blames himself for doing something wrong.

Projections are psychological processes—used to defend against painful feelings, insecurities, negative qualities, wrong-doings, and immoral behaviors. By denying their existence, the narcissist unwittingly attributes them to her partner. Malicious intent is assigned when the partner, himself, has done nothing wrong.

While narcissists project all faults, pleasers automatically blame themselves and internalize the projections of their mate. Pleasers do not trust themselves—to truly know if they have actually offended their mate. In their confusion, doubt, and mistrust of self, they desperately try to figure out how they may have offended their mate—so they can then become aware of their "offensive" behavior and stop doing it.

Hence, the pleaser does do not honestly communicate his feelings. To do so, creates too much risk. Should his narcissistic mate accuse him of cheating simply because he has spoken to a woman at the grocery store, he will stop talking to women to no longer trigger the insecurities of his mate. Accommodation and submission become his only "safe" way of coping.

The risk of confrontation for the purpose of repairing conflict is avoided at all costs. The pleaser accommodates his mate's accusations in order to stop the abuse and sweep it under the carpet. If he admits fault (even though he sometimes knows he has done nothing wrong), the pleaser can temporarily satisfy his mate and stop the abuse. In this manner, his own interpersonal anxiety is temporarily soothed as he essentially manipulates his mate by "agreeing" he was in the wrong.

All of this drama and chaos is repeated over and over again—simply because the narcissist projects all insecurities and all faults onto the pleaser. On his side, he plays into the drama to regain his mate's trust and approval. This is how both the narcissist and pleaser actively avoid solving the problems of their own abusive relationship. Each remains dependent on the other's approval and only the forms of approval-seeking differ. Hence, honest communication (on both sides) does not exist. The pleaser does not dare confront his mate's accusations because of the risk of additional abuse or abandonment.

The pleaser has not yet learned to set and hold boundaries. He still assumes he is somehow responsible for his mate's aggressive behavior. Hence, he actively regulates his narcissistic mate's feelings and behavior—by "agreeing" and modifying his own. Essentially, the pleaser morphs himself into whoever she wants him to be, agreeing with her at all times, at the expense of himself.

The narcissist and pleaser manipulate each another in different ways to compensate for their internal feelings of inadequacy, mistrust, and and worthlessness—and both fail to see their role in the creation and toleration of their trauma bond. Invariably, the pleaser becomes exhausted regulating his mate's neediness and paranoia, eventually running out of steam.

Within these insecure dynamics, the abuse has no resolve. Willing to compromise himself for the sake of ending an abusive attack, the pleaser will agree (through submission or accommodation) to some crime he has not committed. Essentially, he conveys (manipulating through accommodation): *It Is Me—and I'll do whatever you wish, so you are no longer mad at me.* He then morphs himself into whoever she needs him to be—by "agreeing" to accommodate her manipulative accusations.

Hence, the pleaser consciously participates in the false blame-narrative of his mate—that he is the one creating all the problems in the relationship—all to ward off further abuse and regulate her insecurities. Unconsciously, he is simply soothing his own anxiety for the moment and sweeping things under the carpet.

Manipulation and accommodation become the never-ending cycle of the abusive relationship.

Do these interpersonal dynamics sound familiar? Having finally landed an attractive love partner, you may have been surprised how quickly your excitement deteriorated into feelings of intense anxiety—at the thought of screwing up, making mistakes, and losing the woman you had been waiting so long to meet. Possessing little awareness of your deep need to please, you found yourself in a heightened state of anxiety about your ability to keep your mate from either manipulating or abandoning you.

Having worked so hard to please—and to be perfect—you knew you would blame yourself if you screwed things up and she dumped you. Keenly aware of the high stakes involved, you made damn sure to lift her spirits, listen perfectly, and agree with all sorts of judgements and accusations. Unfortunately, what you did not know was the neediness, paranoia and manipulation used to control you were only going to ramp up. Even though you had been doing your best, it was just never enough. As your lover demanded more and more of your time and energy, you eventually ran out of steam—and had nothing left to give. Not possessing the self-esteem to leave, you simply tried harder—making damn sure to agree through accommodation. On your end, you kept thinking you would eventually succeed in convincing her that you were not guilty of the crimes you were being accused of. You hoped you would eventually convince your mate that you were not out to get her.

The above dynamic is the battle of *convincing* both the narcissist and pleaser engage in—for the entire length of the relationship.

Feeling you did not deserve your mate when you met, losing her was not an option. Believing you added no value to your romantic relationship—your value rested in what you could do for your mate and whether you could succeed in keeping her happy.

This brings us to the pleaser's core issues: He has not yet learned to care for himself by communicating his needs, setting and holding boundaries, and remaining true to himself. These skills require the development of self-esteem—and the willingness to stand up for himself. Forever terrified of rejection, conflict, anger, abandonment and abuse, he gives, and gives, and gives—expecting his mate will eventually see all he does and eventually be satisfied. But until such time as the pleaser is *ready* to stand up for himself, he simply gives away his personal power—in favor of seeking the external validation of his narcissistic mate. He does whatever his mate needs him to at the expense of himself to gain her acceptance, approval, and love. This is the pleaser's control—and this is his manipulation. He is *not* being true to himself and does not express his honest feelings about his mate's control and how he feels everything is always twisted back around onto him. Instead, he invariably represses these emotions—by pretending he is okay with her behavior—even though he is clearly not.

As his mate becomes more needful, paranoid and mistrustful, the trauma bond is strengthened—by both the physical aspect of the relationship and the pleaser's willingness to bend over backwards. While the abuse escalates, the physical aspect of the relationship (which is often the primary motivation for remaining in the abusive relationship) remains intact.

Often pregnancies occur early in abusive relationships—which then become hostage takings for pleasers. The control and manipulation are then ramped up—because the narcissist is aware that she has a committed, emotionally-available, soon-to-be father. At this point, any attempt to express a want or a need is immediately twisted back around to make it about her—and what she needs from her mate.

When partners fail to meet their mate's bottomless well of need, they are told:

- "I don't feel supported by you."
- "I'm pregnant and you're not doing a good job taking care of me."
- "You need to be supporting me better.'
- "You are not reliable."
- "If I cannot count on you, how can I trust you to take care of a baby."

Even though these men have been bending over backwards, they are manipulated into believing they are poor partners, uncaring, and soon-to-be incompetent fathers—never doing enough for their insatiable mate. Should they become understandably frustrated or even attempt to stand up for themselves, pleasers are invariably manipulated via accusations:

- "You're always angry."
- "Stop screaming at me."
- "You have anger issues."
- "I think you're an abusive man."

When the partner eventually becomes angry himself—because his feelings, requests, and needs are always twisted back around and made to be about her—he is then threatened:

- "If you don't treat me better, I'm going to have to leave you."
- "How am I going to trust you with a baby when you're abusive towards me?"
- "If you don't want to treat me properly, you don't deserve to raise your child."

Exhausted and confused, partners listen to this type of nonsensical manipulation for months, years, and even decades. Their heads begin to spin and now—because of a pregnancy—they feel increasingly chained to their narcissistic mate. Consistently battered by manipulative words that are devoid of reason, truth, and credibility, pleasers cannot make sense of what is happening in their abusive relationship and why their mate continues to act in the vitriolic and caustic way she does.

Partners find themselves becoming defensive because they are never seen, heard, listened to, or understood. They know they should not be escalating—but they cannot figure out why their girlfriend is having so many problems with them—and why she never seems to listen to what he wants or needs.

Abused men cannot figure their mate out because they are not therapists.

This is why this book was written. Each of the chapters will provide specific information to help you see what you are up against, reduce your interpersonal anxiety, and teach you what you need to know about your abusive relationship—including the skills you will need to escape your chains of pleasing.

This chapter has discussed how abusive relationships are formed and strengthened. The purpose was to demonstrate the significant role the pleaser plays in the formation, development, and cycle of his own abuse. If the partner is to reclaim his personal power and develop self-worth, he must learn to tolerate and soothe his own interpersonal anxiety—and see it is not him causing his own abuse.

True freedom, self-esteem, happiness, and authentic power are developed by accepting responsibility for the choices (and mistakes) you have made—and learning from them—as opposed to ignoring reality and trivializing an extremely dangerous relationship. As you read on, you will come to see that you have choices and opportunities before you—

to pivot and do something productive about your abusive relationship. But before this can happen, you must begin to acknowledge your reality—that your abusive relationship is only getting worse—as your mate's control and manipulation intensify. There is **nothing** you can do to fix or save your relationship.

> If you do not plan to escape, the relationship *will* eventually implode—and your mate may very well leave, press false criminal charges, and attempt to withhold your children.

As you begin to open your eyes—and take a sobering look at your abusive relationship—you can begin the process of differentiation (which is the active process of developing self-awareness, creating invisible boundaries, and managing the anxiety that results from potential conflict, rejection, and abuse). By learning to challenge and frustrate your strong need to seek your mate's approval, your need to please is released over time—as you begin to regulate your own emotions—without re-engaging. Know that you are in no way responsible for making your mate angry or causing your mate's unstable reactions in any way.

You can begin to challenge yourself and frustrate your need to please by no longer allowing yourself to get "sucked in" to conversations designed to control and manipulate you. When you acknowledge that your feelings and needs will never be heard—*ever*—and your attempt at verbal boundaries will never be respected, you can accept that engaging, explaining, justifying, and proving yourself—is futile. Should you decide to begin this process of differentiation, disengagement, and frustrating your need to please—you are, in essence, taking the very first steps towards respecting and trusting yourself, owning your own interpersonal anxiety, and beginning the powerful process of letting go.

This decision is empowering! It marks the beginning of reclaiming your

personal power—by owning and protecting your own feelings. This marks a powerful step towards the development of self-awareness and self-esteem!

Of course, you are not about to inform your mate about these internal shifts that you are making. You will be challenging and beginning to frustrate your need to please—instead of engaging in unstable interactions with your mate. You will instead focus on becoming aware each time you seek to please. Instead of stepping in and engaging—you simply disengage and make up an excuse that you need to be somewhere or do something important.

When you stop giving your mate's perceptions, feelings, and words credibility—releasing your need to please becomes possible. You will soon learn to understand that all of her insecurities and wrong-doings are merely projections of herself.

This process of getting honest with yourself (while protecting your feelings from your mate) marks the first major step of standing up to the bully (that just happens to be your girlfriend or wife). This initial process involves getting real with yourself—by acknowledging that you are in an abusive relationship that will only intensify in frequency and duration—until implosion. All the hope, rationalizations, and excuses in the world are not going to bend this reality.

In order to develop self-awareness and self-esteem, you are ultimately responsible for learning to stand up for yourself and put yourself first.

Know that you are responsible for your own feelings and behavior. You are not responsible for the feelings and behavior of your mate.

Internal strength and power is developed by owning, regulating, and soothing your own painful emotions. As you own your interpersonal anxiety—and begin to disengage (when and wherever possible)—you begin to frustrate your insecurities by no longer feeding them.

Eventually, you uproot these insecurities and begin to sever your trauma bond. Hence, you protect yourself from manipulative attacks (without so much as saying a word).

No longer will you deny the permanence of your own abuse—by rationalizing your romantic relationship will one day get better—and that you can somehow get her to listen to you. Now staring reality in the face, you begin to look at real options before you—and acknowledge that you are going to have to get out of your abusive relationship—no matter how hard it might be.

The pursuit of true freedom, happiness, and authentic power requires significant courage and dedication to reality.

Breathe deeply. Don't panic. There is far more to learn, practice, and plan for—before you will be *ready* to escape the chains of your abusive relationship.

In the following chapter, you will learn what drives your mate's aggression—and subsequent manipulation—and will come to see it has nothing to do with you. Once you develop this emotional awareness (your next level of self-esteem), you will come to accept you cannot change or help your mate who has no desire to change. You will come to accept you cannot *get* or *make* her listen to how you feel—or see who you really are.

By stepping back and doing this emotional work on yourself, you begin to trust your perceptions and feelings over those of your narcissistic mate's. No longer do you put the needs and feelings of your mate before your own. This difficult internal transition marks the beginning of disengaging—by respecting, trusting, and taking care of yourself. This is a game-changer!

Remember—you have free will. You have choices and options before you. You are never stuck in an abusive relationship, even though you may have convinced yourself that you are. There is only one person you can change—and only one person you must ultimately care for—**You!**

Pleasing is manipulative and transactional. It is giving to get. It is bending over backwards—at the expense of yourself. Pleasers tend to believe that being *kind* to others will make other people like them. It does not. In their willful pursuit of external power, pleasers actively avoid owning and regulating their own emotions—in the hope that they can get their mate's approval and love—via accommodation and submission.

You can no longer afford to ignore your mental health in the hope you can gain the love of a toxic woman who has no love within herself to give.

3

Anger:
A Flight From Responsibility

Covert anger can be difficult to recognize. When many think of a person who is angry, they often tend to associate such behaviors with yelling, screaming, and physical abuse. More often than not, narcissistic women are covertly angry—at least in the early stages of an abusive relationship. Piercing glares, defensive reactions, viscous words—are certainly not yelling and screaming. Yet these behaviors still originate from the emotion of anger. The subtle aggression from a narcissist is often covert.

Chronic irritability and unstable mood swings are the most easily recognizable emotions of a narcissistic woman. The narcissist's anger is a massive defense mechanism—to protect against painful feelings of worthlessness, guilt, shame, rejection, betrayal, and perceived persecution. Her covert aggression is always justified to be the fault of the partner—for "provoking" or "attacking" her—when he has done nothing of the sort.

As a child, your narcissistic mate was exposed to frequent aggressive and manipulative power plays by authority figures in her life. She protected herself by freezing—or shutting down. Your mate was not permitted to be herself—or make mistakes of any kind. She remained invisible and learned to bury her emotions—deep below the surface of consciousness—to emotionally survive the crushing weight of control, aggression, and manipulation she endured in her home. Frequently the target of shame-inducing rants, your mate would freeze—to protect herself from parental aggression and manipulation during these vulnerable and formative years.

Eventually, during adolescence, your mate could take no more—and began to fight back—to defend herself against parental aggression. By then, she had lost all confidence in herself, and became extremely critical and mistrustful of both herself and her parents. She came to feel ugly, flawed, and deeply inadequate within—and now holds deep feelings of hate towards herself—and towards her parents for what they did to her. Feeling deep bitterness for the way she was treated—your mate has become cynical and mistrustful of others—as if others are out to get her.

The pleaser must learn how his angry mate thinks—if he is to protect himself from her hate-filled words—and do something productive about his abusive reality. He must understand what **causes** his mate's anger and volatility. Once he can see how deep her pathology lies, he becomes determined to detach from his hope that one day she might change.

The pleaser must also heal his own trust issues. He frequently gives his mate the benefit of the doubt, feels sorry for her, and hopes he will one day break through his hostile mate's defenses and get her to see he is not trying to hurt her.

The pleaser blames himself (often on an unconscious or emotional level) for causing his mate's aggression. When she reacts with angry, hate-filled words, he feels a sudden loss of power within himself because of an impending attack. Feeling as though he is somehow responsible for the feelings and behaviors of his narcissistic mate, he does not trust himself to know his mate's angry words about him are not true.

> Neither the pleaser nor the narcissist can independently trust their own perceptions and feelings about who is ultimately causing the conflict in the abusive relationship and, as a result, desperately seeks the agreement and validation from the other.

Often at the center of the narcissistic attack are the implications that the partner is malicious or untrustworthy. The pleaser, on the other hand, believes he can eventually convince his mate he is reliable and trustworthy. Yet, knowing his mate will not accept confrontation of any kind, he attempts to convince her that he did not intend, say, or do what she insists he intended, said, or did.

Unfortunately, a chronically angry individual will never admit to being wrong—because to admit fault, would prove that she is "worthless." Hence, the pleaser lives in a never-ending cycle of abuse—defending himself, and hoping to convince his mate that he is trustworthy and not behaving in the malicious manner he is so often accused of.

The narcissist has no self-awareness or emotional intelligence. Forever claiming moral virtue, she believes she is always right and would never lie about anything. The narcissist feels she has the right to point out the "faults" of others and sees her insulting words as a strength. Frequently paranoid, she believes her partner is disloyal and often up to no good. Her lack of self-awareness, combined with her unwillingness to accept responsibility for her malicious words and behaviors, creates an extremely deceptive and manipulative reality. In turn, her manipulation causes the pleaser to second-guess himself about whether he can trust his own perceptions, feelings, and experiences.

> **The pleaser must learn to trust his own perceptions, feelings, and experiences over that of his narcissistic mate. He must learn to put himself first—and no longer give credibility to the false perceptions and manipulative words of his mate.**

By understanding how his covertly angry mate thinks, and learning to trust he is not causing her anger in any way, the pleaser can begin to let go of his hope for a favorable outcome with his mate.

A chronically irritable or angry individual remains stuck in a victim mentality. Growing up, compliance and submission were the order of the day. When she expressed herself, she would frequently be squashed with manipulative and demeaning words. She was conditioned to believe that her parents' anger—meant that she was "wrong" about her opinions, values, desires, and beliefs. She was taught that difference or disagreements (autonomy) would not be tolerated. She was attacked with the inherent, manipulative message that she was "stupid," "disgusting," or "wrong" for having differing opinions, beliefs, and feelings from her parents. As a young girl, she was abused simply for being herself.

Now, as a traumatized adult, your mate remains frozen, shut down, and bitter because she was conditioned to believe she was "wrong" about so many things she was *not* actually wrong about. The trauma she experienced as a child caused significant internal anguish, conflicting beliefs, confusion, and self-loathing. Your mate now has an inaccurate, deceptive view of herself—what she is worth and what she believes she deserves from a love partner.

Feeling as though she has been "ripped off" from loving parents, your mate believes she has had it so much worse than others. Had she had emotionally-available parents who showed her love—and accepted her for who she was—she would have inherited more confidence and self-esteem. Had she been treated better, she would not have had to endure the humiliating and terrifying beat-downs she experienced as a young girl—and life would not have been so difficult and unfair. She now blames her parents for her internal feelings of inadequacy and self-loathing, believing these self-critical feelings are who she really is.

The angry individual is not aware that she is responsible for healing her trauma and feelings of self-loathing. She questions why should she should have to do the hard work of healing, when she was a victim of abuse. According to her, this is just another extreme injustice.

Feeling cursed for the loveless childhood she was forced to endure, the angry individual feels denied the confidence she wishes she had and assumes most others possess. Unconsciously, she feels like a worthless piece of garbage—and lives in fear her partner will see through her mask of righteousness and ultimately reject her—unaware that it is she who is ultimately rejecting herself. She attempts to hide from herself (and others) in ego and a false persona of moral virtue. But because her arrogant personality is fake, the angry individual can only remain stable so long as her partner is behaving just as she expects and needs him to behave.

The pleaser is expected to provide all of the love and support his mate missed out on as a child and still craves. According to her, his job is to take care of all her emotional and unmet developmental needs.

Your mate learned that mistakes, or the smallest of imperfections, resulted in abuse—often followed with punitive consequences. When she was not able to meet her parents' unrealistic expectations, she was manipulated and shamed to believe she had done something humiliating, wrong, or stupid. To ultimately protect herself from these frequent parental admonishments, she would emotionally freeze, shut down, and repress her emotions deep within.

The narcissist now remains emotionally shut down and invulnerable. Still traumatized from childhood, she believes the answer to her prayers lies in the hands of a love partner. To protect against deep feelings of inadequacy and insecurity, she resides in ego and a fragile persona of moral virtue, righteousness, and entitlement.

Behind her thinly-veiled persona of moral virtue, remains a fragile, traumatized little girl—who easily becomes triggered by her partner's differences and individuality. Anger begets anger. Just as her parents were triggered by her autonomy as a child, she is now triggered by her partner's autonomy in her romantic relationship. Because of her own abuse as a child, she has become abusive.

> Just like his narcissistic counterpart, the pleaser has wounds resulting from childhood trauma. Unlike his mate who rebelled to protect herself, he conformed and complied to emotionally survive childhood. Doing what he was told to do was never questioned. Hence, the pleaser now seeks the approval of his narcissistic mate, just as he did his parents. For both, validation is critical to obtaining feelings of stability and security.

Unfortunately, the pleaser will rarely be validated in his abusive relationship. Unaware of the breadth and depth of his mate's narcissistic personality disorder, he attempts to convince himself that he can "get" his girlfriend or wife to listen and understand him—and that he will eventually be successful in this pursuit. This explains why the pleaser finds himself "stuck" in the deceptive psychological reality of his abusive mate. Only her wants and needs matter. Conversely, he is not permitted to have his own feelings and needs.

To no longer personalize her abusive words, the pleaser must learn where his mate's anger originates. His mate's instability and aggression are caused by deep insecurities—in which she takes everything personally—and projects her paranoia and trumped-up accusations onto him. Once the pleaser can see through his mate's anger and projections—he develops the self-esteem to know it is ***not*** him causing his own abuse.

It is at this point in therapy, that clients feel more confident and trusting within themselves. Once they reach this level of self-esteem, many now inform me:

- "I can now see why she's getting angry."
- "I'm more confident in my perceptions and feelings now."
- "I know it is not me."
- "I know how unreasonable and insecure she is."
- "There's no point in engaging."
- "She never listens to me—I can now see why."
- "She just literally makes things up."

Seeing your mate's anger to be the result of trauma and a victim mentality offers a great deal of relief—as opposed to believing that it is you causing your mate's aggression. This new level of self-esteem marks a renewed determination.

> Recognizing your chronically irritable mate to be the highly insecure, unstable, manipulative, and angry woman that she is—changes your perception about how reasonable, intelligent, and credible you once believed her to be.

Both you and your narcissistic mate have been looking outside of yourselves for love—specifically in your romantic relationship. To begin severing your trauma bond, you must learn you are not responsible for the feelings of your mate. Now that you know that it is not ***you*** causing your mate's caustic moods—you must accept the responsibility that it ***is*** you participating in your own abuse—by engaging in interpersonal discussions with a traumatized, insecure, and irrational woman—hoping to one day be seen, heard, and understood.

Until you can get to this level of self-esteem, you will repeatedly engage in a battle of convincing—in which you both try to convince the other of who is doing what to whom. Then, after another abusive beat-down, you invariably return to second-guessing yourself once again:

- "I have been getting pissed off."
- "She seems convinced I am the one who is abusive."
- "She always seems so sure of herself—like she truly believes what she's saying."
- "Maybe I am wrong?"
- "Maybe it is me—and I'm projecting my own crap onto her?"
- "Maybe I'm in denial about my own anger issues?"
- "Maybe it is me who is abusive."

This is the mental insanity partners experience on a regular basis with an angry girlfriend or wife who never accepts responsibility. For the narcissist, compliance, submission, loyalty, and continual presence are all proof of your love—and what she requires to remain stable. Should you not see things her way and agree with her insulting words about you (or anyone you love, for that matter), your mate will insist that you *do* see things her way—through any aggressive, manipulative means necessary—to coerce your agreement and regain your loyalty.

Your mate needs your submission—to trust her own perceptions—because she has no ability to independently trust herself. She cannot trust her perceptions without your validation. Your mate's underlying aggression is ultimately her defense mechanism—to defend against feeling excruciatingly painful emotions.

Ultimately, your mate feels that she has been denied the ease, rights, and privileges so many others have been afforded—and instead, been forced to live in an unjust world without the recognition and love she deserves. Consciously, or unconsciously, she now hates her parents for the injustice of their persecution.

Your mate needs you to behave in the precise manner she insists you behave—to avoid experiencing her deep insecurities and fears.

Living in ego—in her thinly veiled mask of moral virtue, your mate does not see herself as angry. Instead, she sees herself as a passionate, strong, and determined woman—who feels justified in rebelling against the persecution of an unjust world full of "stupid," "incompetent" people. She has no awareness of how critical she is or that she is powerless to control or change anyone else. Hence, she runs around pushing her hate-filled agenda—and trying to change others into who she needs them to be—feeling justified in doing so.

Because she is blind to her judgements of self and others—she creates a false reality of what she assumes others are thinking and feeling about her. Feeling overlooked and persecuted, she believes her judgements to be one hundred percent accurate—as if there is no other reality except hers—and others have no right to defend their reality.

Ironically, at the same time, your mate desperately requires your approval so she can trust her own reality. Blind to herself, she does not see her judgmental and critical nature to be a problem. Unaware of her aggression and manipulation, she is mystified why people react in the manner they do—and, as a result, feels further victimized and persecuted.

Deep down, your mate is jealous of you—of your happiness, success, and friendships. She is competitive with you, and cannot seem to figure out why things rarely work out for her. Your mate is jealous of the love you give freely to others and so "sparsely" to her. In her myriad of judgements, she sees you and your loved ones to be "unhealthy" and "flawed." Then, even when your mate has you all to herself, she bashes you for your "unhealthy" attachments to the "horrible" people you associate with.

Living in ego, your mate has no empathy or compassion for herself or others—and she cannot develop empathy and compassion until (or unless) she begins the process of reversing the mirror and looking at herself.

But self-reflection and personal growth require effort, insight, and compassion. Your mate cannot develop insight because she remains externally focused and perceives *people* to be the problem. She expects love, understanding, and respect from others—even though she does not respect herself or others. It is people who are the problem. It is they who need to be confronted—so they can see the error of their ways and take responsibility for their actions.

Ironically, the narcissist demands accountability from the world—while she herself detests the notion of personal responsibility. Because she believes life has wronged her, she now believes that life *owes* her. Until the narcissist is ready to confront her defense mechanism of anger (and many never do), she will remain bitter about an unjust world—in which she feels cheated and persecuted, while others have had it so much easier than her.

The narcissist believes she is enlightened, even though she gossips and complains relentlessly. She is angry that people do not behave the way she expects them to—and for not changing once she has told them what they need to do. If they would only accept responsibility for their "stupidity" and "faulty nature," the narcissist could fix the world and make people better—without ever having to fix herself.

And here she remains, fully distracted and opposed to the world not being the way she wants it to be.

**The angry individual, just like the pleaser, has not learned that she does
not have the power to change other people—nor is she aware of how
frequently she sabotages herself. According to her, she is not responsible
to heal her own trauma—because things are never her fault.**

In the end, the narcissist requires some significant catalyst (or wake-up call) to stop fighting for external power—and accept she cannot change or control others. This crisis must be one that involves some severe threat of loss—like a job or a love partner. But in the face of such loss, in which she must make a decision to keep her mouth shut or experience a loss she herself has created, the narcissist will usually choose the latter—always fighting against the perceived injustice of a world she herself is creating.

Should the narcissist confront her feelings of persecution—and breach her defense mechanism of anger—she *can* painfully work through her feelings of powerlessness and the massive sense of injustice she feels. This is an extremely painful process—in which she must confront significant feelings of betrayal and injustice.

**Often, this crisis of powerlessness occurs at the fall-out stage of the abusive
relationship—at the time of separation. Because of extreme feelings
of hate, betrayal, fear, and persecution within, the narcissist goes on a
campaign of revenge against her partner—for having dared to "persecute"
her—even though it is she who is persecuting and abandoning him.**

When her partner escapes (or even when she implodes) and then criminally charges him, the narcissist remains angry, vengeful, and righteously indignant—as if her partner has ruined her life and deserves to be punished.

**Until the narcissist feels her painful emotions underneath her
anger (and no longer acts on them), she will not be able to exercise
compassion for herself—or others. In other words, she cannot**

develop the emotion of empathy. The pleaser, himself, cannot make his own massive internal transition—until he learns to stand up for himself, put himself first, and step into all that he fears.

For the pleaser to make his own massive internal shift from the powerlessness of pleasing, he must accept he has no power to change his angry mate—or get through to her by submitting or accommodation. To make this psychological shift, he must finally arrive at his own moment of truth—or "sweet spot" of acceptance—in which he must acknowledge that his mate will never see or hear him—and that the only healthy, reasonable, or responsible choice he has is to escape his abusive relationship.

Hopefully, you feel a new level of confidence that IT IS NOT YOU causing your mate's anger, instability, and abusive attacks. However, you ARE participating in your abusive relationship by pleasing, tolerating, enabling, and choosing to stay.

You may want to ask yourself, "What are the rewards of making this decision to escape?" The following are just a few of the powerful reasons to make this decision:

- Reclaiming your lost self—and healing past trauma
- Developing self-respect and trust in yourself
- Learning to self-reflect and release your need to please
- Letting go of the belief you can change another
- Building self-worth, internal strength, and learning to like, trust, and respect yourself
- Providing yourself, and your children, with an emotionally-available parent—at least half of the time.

When you accept that your narcissist mate will never see you, hear you, understand you, care for you, or accept responsibility for her immoral words and behaviors, then (and only then) are you ready to accept you must disengage and make the courageous decision to let go.

This is life inside a narcissistic relationship. Should you see yourself in these dynamics, a major psychological shift is now in order. This shift is more than possible! I am about to demonstrate the powerful strategy of recognizing coercive manipulation. Once you can recognize the various forms of coercive manipulation, it is a game changer. You will then be able to see through the invisible abuse that is coercive manipulation— and once you do, you will develop more trust in yourself than you could ever have imagined.

4

Living a Lie:
Recognizing Coercive Manipulation

Your narcissist girlfriend or wife uses different forms of coercive manipulation to steal your personal power—and leave you feeling confused, humiliated, and second-guessing yourself. Without knowing how to recognize the different forms of manipulation, you remain vulnerable and unable to make sense of your deceptive reality. But there is *real hope*. Once you can see each of these common forms, you will come to trust yourself and develop a new level of self-esteem.

As a pleaser, learning to trust yourself—and guard against your deceptive reality—requires that you recognize all common forms of manipulation. You must ultimately learn *it is not you* causing the conflict in your hostile, dependent relationship—even though your mate most certainly insists it is. Once you can clearly see the manipulation, you can learn to avoid the many manipulative power plays that ultimately suck you in.

Once you recognize the various forms of manipulation, you can come to accept that engagement is futile.

Living in an abusive relationship, you never know when—or where—the next attack is coming. Hence, you have learned to keep your feelings and opinions to yourself—to protect yourself and ward off attacks.

You have learned to keep yourself in self-protection mode which looks and feels the following way:

- "If I don't do what she wants, she'll attack and beat me down—often in front of the kids."
- "It is getting harder to get back up again."
- "She's threatened to take the kids and leave. There is no way I could live without them."
- "She could actually call the police one day—and accuse me of doing something I did not do. I know damn well she is capable of this."
- "I have no choice but to keep my mouth shut."

This type of fear-based thinking has likely become your reality. The terror injected by each manipulative attack beats you back into submission—or invokes fear about how your mate might punish you. Frequently on guard—and keeping your thoughts to yourself—you live in fear of the very real possibility that one day your mate will make good on her threats—and potentially phone the police and accuse you of assaulting her—or leave with the children and keep them from you.

Because of the terror of life inside an abusive relationship, all partners absolutely need to know the following: The psychological and emotional consequences of remaining in an abusive relationship—and tolerating the intensifying, manipulative beat-downs, create a heightened state of confusion and chronic anxiety—that some have referred to as "fog."

At the same time, resilience to the abuse deteriorates—one blistering attack after another. Soon, men feel as if they are losing their mind.

Hence, the longer you stay, the more weakened and defeated you feel. Your submission is fueled by the very real possibility that something unimaginable and devastating could happen at any time—should you dare to be yourself. Terror of an impending attack keeps you in a chronic state of anxiety, disarray—and even defeat—as you consider what your mate is capable of doing:

- *Will she withhold the kids?*
- *Will she kick me out of my own home?*
- *Will she charge me with some conjured up accusations?*

These fears, and the very real possibility of them happening, are enough to cause a nervous breakdown—or worse. Hence, you may well feel stuck in the powerless position of submission.

In reality, you are abusing yourself—as your parents abused you—and just as your mate now abuses you. In the same manner you survived childhood, you are now attempting to survive your abusive relationship. This is your trauma.

The abuse will stop—only when you decide to stop it *or* when the inevitable implosion occurs—as we are about to observe in the following chapter. Hence, it is critical that you continue to build confidence and recognize the various forms of coercive manipulation. This process is critical—if you are to ultimately develop the trust in yourself and renew your determination to escape.

We will begin by looking at the most obvious forms of coercive manipulation, beginning with blame, accusations, threats, and exploitation.

PART I: BLAME, ACCUSATIONS, THREATS AND EXPLOITATION

Blame and Accusations:

Your narcissistic mate is forever blaming and accusing you for causing her vitriolic reactions. In her never-ending flight from responsibility, she assigns malicious motives, words, and actions to you—her convenient scapegoat.

You must learn to recognize blame and accusations to be the manipulative power plays they are. Otherwise, you will emotionally internalize your mate's manipulation and get "sucked in" to her abusive narrative. In so doing, you will continue to defend, explain, or prove yourself—hoping to eventually convince her that you did not say what she insists you said, or do what she says you did.

Only wounded (or traumatized) individuals with personality disorders, manipulate their partners—to deflect against owning their own faults, feelings, and wrongdoings. Blame and accusations are just one way they accomplish this.

Those motivated towards personal growth look inside themselves and seek to learn from their faults, reactions, and mistakes—thereby eradicating the fault from within. In this way, healthy individuals use their faults and mistakes to consciously develop and grow throughout the course of their lives.

Conversely, narcissists are only interested in finding faults in others. Hence, partners are often accused of a variety of immoral behaviors, including cheating, assault, sexual abuse, and wanting to harm their children—all of which could not be farther from the truth. Most, if not all, blame and accusations stem from the narcissist's defense mechanisms that serve the purpose of avoiding painful emotions—by deflecting or projecting responsibility and attributing fault to the partner. Accusations are destructive and dangerous because they are often followed by threats.

Threats and Exploitation:

Threats tend to illicit terror. Hence, are probably the most powerful form of coercive manipulation. Threats ensure that you do as you are told—or risk losing what you cannot image living without—specifically, your children, career, and freedom.

Should you have children with your narcissistic girlfriend or wife (as many men do), your children become your world. And guess who knows this? Hence, the children are used as pawns to ensure submission. Know that threats are not always stated directly—and can often come in the form of accusations:

- "I think you're a negligent father."
- "You're putting the children at risk."
- "I think you're touching the baby inappropriately."
- "You assaulted me so I don't trust you with the kids. They aren't safe."

Emotionally-available fathers who love their children are accused of all manner of abusive behavior. Obviously, with such terrifying accusations—and underlying threats, the narcissist can exert a tremendous amount of crushing control when this type of insidious manipulation is used. Forced to choose between submission—or seeing their children every day, many make the mistake of choosing the former. And do not think for a moment I would suggest you abandon your children. I am, however, suggesting that you lawyer up before you plan to escape. Too often, under this type of duress, fathers rationalize staying "for the sake of the children"—too terrified to take the risks associated with escape. This strategy is likely to backfire.

Threats and accusations are extremely painful and psychologically destructive. In a split second, they cause an immediate hemorrhaging of power—as the partner is left shocked by what he is being accused of—and what terrifying loss he may have to face. For example, the threat that your mate will leave and take the children (because of an accusation you are wanting to harm them) and the thought of having to defend against criminal charges strikes unspeakable terror in you. This level of fear, in and of itself, fuels the compulsion to submit—just to make the threats (and ultimately your terror) stop.

While submission might work for a period of time, you must know that your mate will (in all likelihood) make good on her threats. I have seen too many men place their hope in submission—that it will will eventually buy stability. It does not! These men would have been far better off beating their narcissistic mate to the punch—and escaping without her knowing what hit her.

When an emotionally available father is threatened with the loss of his children, he will do anything to prevent this from happening. Hence, he may choose the path of submission—and "take it like a man." However, it is not recommended to remain in a "hostage-taking" to assuage fears of losing your children—only to be abandoned and have to fight for custody at a later date.

The fight is coming whether you like it or not! The custody proceedings may not be avoidable. Hence, sacrificing your mental health (and that of your children) will not prevent the inevitable implosion and potential custody proceedings down the road.

You may want to ask yourself the question: Is it wise to submit—and wait for your mate to implode—or would it be far more prudent to lawyer up and plan your escape?

In all my years of private practice—working with men and women in abusive relationships—not once have I discovered a person who was truly "trapped." In reality, pleasers trap themselves—in their attempt to avoid the critical decision to leave—to avoid confronting their fears of abandonment, letting go, and the unknown.

I see far too many pleasers shrink in the face of their abusive nightmare—as they attempt to avoid the only sane choice before them. Crippled with fear, they anticipate their abuse will ramp up should they make the decision to leave and—in some cases it does—but the abuse is *not* permanent *after* separation. Remaining in an abusive relationship is a recipe for utter defeat. While threats and accusations are obviously terrifying, living under this type of duress—with a terrorist who is more than comfortable exploiting you—is a recipe for disaster.

You must decide if you can accept the reality that your abuse is never going to stop until you stop it—or your mate implodes.

PART II: JUDGEMENT AND CRITICIZING

Many partners are not aware that judgment and criticism constitute manipulation. Often when they are judged, pleasers assume that the judgements from their mate are accurate. More often than not, they are assumptions or projections.

Frequently, your narcissistic mate takes your intentions, words, and behavior out of context—and makes some assumption (judgement) before expressing it critically. Should you feel hurt or demeaned in any way, she may react with a childish rationalization, such as "Well, it's the truth"—as if making critical judgments are appropriate—so long as they happen to be true. Like the petulant child she is, your mate feels justified making critical remarks insofar as she believes them to be true.

With righteous indignancy, you are criticized for some perceived lack—such as appearance, intelligence, morality, kindness, or mental health—while, at the same time, she arrogantly tells you how "attractive," "intelligent," "moral," "kind," and "healthy" she is—as if demeaning you and assigning false virtue to herself is somehow virtuous. When you learn that judgments and criticism are, in fact, manipulation, you are less likely to take them personally.

Each judgment or criticism sends the implicit message that your reactions are the problem—and not your mate's abuse. Obviously, the manipulation is painful and causes you to doubt yourself: *Maybe she does have the right to confront me and maybe I am being too emotional.*

In a split second, you have been lied to twice:
  (1)   You have been told (manipulated) that you have been "confronted" when, in fact, you have been judged and criticized—a difference worth noting.
  (2)   You have been told (manipulated) that you have no right to feel hurt or demeaned after being criticized—that your mate is merely "communicating" in a healthy manner—and again, that your reactions are the problem.

You may have attempted to call your mate out in the past, only to have your perceptions and feelings denied, as she instantly reacts, "What? I am just telling the truth." Obviously, being judgmental in a romantic relationship is not kind or respectful. Judgements objectify you—by sending the message you are not worthy of your mate.

Ironically, judgements and criticism are often defense mechanisms—in which the narcissist projects unconscious judgements of herself.

When you can see that blame, accusations, threats, exploitation, judgement, and criticism are all forms of coercive manipulation—you can recognize the defense mechanisms of your mate—used to avoid deep feelings of worthlessness and self-loathing. Knowing this, you can now understand how inadequate and insecure your mate feels about herself—and precisely why she is judging or criticizing you.

PART III: DENIAL, DISCOUNTING, ORDERING, BLOCKING, DIVERTING, DEFLECTING AND FORGETTING

The following forms of manipulation tend to be more subtle than those we have already discussed, yet each have the same purpose of deflecting responsibility and protecting the narcissist from feeling painful emotions.

> **Unconsciously, your mate does not believe she deserves you—and manipulates you for the purpose of feeling better about herself.**

Denial

Denial is a common form of manipulation used to steal personal power and maintain control. Many don't recognize denial to be manipulation—and tend to see it as a legitimate way of communicating. It is not. Denial offers no information—and simply shuts a conversation down. Observe the following responses:

- "That's not true."
- "That's not what happened."
- "I did not say that."

Just like that (in the middle of what seemed to be a normal conversation), your reality is denied. Should you feel shocked, confused, insulted, demeaned, or controlled by your mate's denial—and feel certain that she did, in fact, say what you know she said—or did, in fact, do what you know she did, your mate will react defensively—using childish rationalizations:

- "It's true."
- "I didn't do that."
- "You're making that up."
- "You never said that."
- "What are you getting mad about?"
- "You're getting upset over nothing."
- "I'm not angry."
- "I'm not abusive."
- "I never did anything wrong."

Denial is the basis of an abusive relationship. When your reality is frequently denied, it becomes difficult to remember what was actually said in a previous conversation—or whether something actually happened in a previous situation. Denial instills doubt and confusion—that perhaps things were not the way you remember them to be. When you are manipulated to question your reality (via manipulative denial), you are forced to wrestle with the doubt that something did, in fact, happen the way you remember it happening—or the possibility that it may not have happened the way you remember it happening.

It is difficult to comprehend how an individual can look you in the eyes—and insist that something that actually happened—did not happen. It is difficult to comprehend that an individual can believe an obvious misrepresentation of the truth. It is difficult to comprehend how someone can be so blatantly dishonest—to seemingly convince herself of anything that casts her in a positive light.

The narcissistic has the uncanny ability to deflect any perceived fault, wrong-doing, or guilty behavior—by using a variety of dishonest and manipulative methods of communication. She can convince herself that something that actually happened, did not happen. It is difficult to comprehend how dishonest one has to be within themselves to be capable of doing this.

But remember, the narcissist is a proficient liar—and is constantly deceiving herself—to avoid accepting responsibility and holding herself accountable.

Discounting

Discounting is a defense mechanism that constitutes manipulation. It is difficult to detect—and instills feelings of inadequacy, doubt, anxiety, and confusion. When your mate talks to you about what you have accomplished—as if it was worthless or means nothing—your efforts and accomplishments are being discounted.

Partners are often shocked, hurt, or confused when their feelings or efforts are discounted—especially when they have been bending over backwards to please their mate—only to hear:
- "You don't spend enough time with me."
- "You're so inconsistent with your love."
- "You're not dependable."
- "How can I trust you with the kids?"

Just like that (out of the blue), you are attacked—and your feelings, efforts, and and energy are discounted—and then followed up with judgmental or critical attacks. More lies about you—all designed to steal your power and take you down to your mate's level. For some reason, you never seem to be doing enough, trying hard enough, or being dependable enough. Discounting words clash with your subjective reality—of what you know you have been doing for your mate and how hard you have been trying.

You may wonder how your narcissistic mate cannot see how much you are doing for her. You may often wonder where she comes up with such crazy perceptions about you. Just like every other form of manipulation, discounting sends the message that you are deficient, inadequate, or worthless as a love partner—or that you are not honest enough, doing enough, spending enough time, or trying hard enough.

Should you attempt to communicate your hurt or frustration, your feelings are sure to be denied:

- "That's not true."
- "You haven't been trying."
- "Don't lie to me."

Discounting sends the implicit message that you have no right to feel the way you do.

Should you not recognize that your feelings and efforts are frequently discounted and why—and that your mate's words are, in fact, manipulation—you are likely to spend hours, days, weeks, and even years doubting how it is that you frequently come across in such an offensive or unlovable manner—and how it is you keep "failing" as a love partner. Discounting erodes your self-worth—about the value you bring to your relationship and your ability to trust your own perceptions, feelings, experiences, and reality. *Maybe I am just a shitty person? Maybe something is seriously wrong with me? Maybe I am unlovable?*

After months, years, or decades of manipulation, how could you not end up thinking this way? Who you are and what you bring to relationship, is frequently under assault—from the various forms of manipulation and lies you hear on a regular basis. Subjecting yourself to a manipulative individual only reinforces your own feelings of worthlessness—resulting from unresolved trauma, pleasing, morphing, earning, and editing yourself (walking on eggshells) for as long as you can remember.

Ordering

Ordering is an easy form of manipulation to detect—and sends the explicit message that you had better do as you are told—or else. The "or else" is what instills terror of further abuse or the threat of punishment—should the order not be obeyed.

Your narcissistic girlfriend or wife is not about to ask for what she needs. Asking questions requires vulnerability and the capacity to regulate difficult emotions. Your mate cannot regulate her feelings of disappointment should she not get her way. Hence, she must bark orders—to prevent you from saying "No" or expressing your own autonomy. Your mate does not have the internal strength to feel disappointment without feeling angry. Hence, her control is her ongoing attempt to avoid these painful emotions.

> **Your narcissistic mate is not aware that she herself is responsible for the regulation of her own feelings. Conversely, she firmly believes it is YOUR job to regulate her feelings.**

For the narcissist, asking is not possible—because it permits the partner to have his own autonomy. Autonomy and equality cannot be tolerated because she would then have to own and be responsible for the regulation of her own difficult feelings—for which she has no power to regulate. Hence, the narcissist remains invulnerable—and barks orders to exert control and steal her partner's personal power.

As you learn to recognize each common form of manipulation and see these power plays for what they are (attempts to steal your power so your mate does not have to feel and experience difficult emotions), you come to understand why your mate behaves the way that she does. All of her manipulations are but defense mechanisms designed to avoid feeling painful emotions that she has not developed the inner strength to feel and regulate.

Blocking, Diverting, or Deflecting

Blocking, diverting, and deflecting are subtle forms of manipulation. They are used to control what can—and cannot—be discussed in the relationship. By controlling all interpersonal communication, the narcissist can remain invulnerable for the purpose of avoiding or tolerating difficult emotions.

In healthy relationships, open communication is used to repair conflict and re-connect. Vulnerability is required to communicate feelings of hurt—and to set a boundary if necessary. Conversely, open communication does not exist in an abusive relationship. The partner's feelings do not matter—primarily because the narcissist does not have the capacity to identify, process, or regulate her own emotions. For this reason, vulnerability and open communication cannot exist in an abusive relationship—and therefore, conflict repair is impossible. Should the partner attempt to confront his mate's control and manipulation, he will be blocked, diverted, or deflected—and his feelings immediately twisted back onto him.

Living in ego (without a shred of emotional awareness), the narcissist's insecurities are protected by defense mechanisms—and impenetrable walls that she has erected to survive the abuse of childhood. Still "frozen"—and guarded behind the fortress of anger she has built around her, she does not have access to many depressive emotions. Frequently feeling attacked, she is immediately triggered—as if the partner had no right to express himself.

Emotional awareness requires self-examination—and a willingness to identify and process your own emotions—to ultimately accept responsibility should you have inadvertently harmed someone. But because the narcissist remains frozen, shut down, and invulnerable, she cannot breach her defense mechanism of anger—and as a result, cannot feel the remorse required to signal she has offended her partner.

In other words, she cannot recognize her manipulative words. In her invulnerable reality, her manipulation is her truth. Unable to accept responsibility because of the shame involved in this process, the narcissist cannot develop emotional intelligence, nor can she learn to tolerate difficult emotions without becoming defensive. She simply lacks the capacity to feel uncomfortable emotions without her defenses being triggered. Hence, she cannot breach her defense mechanisms—to gain insight and see she is manipulative. Blocking is simply another defense mechanism used to protect herself from feeling her emotions.

Your mate can block you without so much as a word. A sneer, a glare, a look of disgust, or a smug little grin is all that is required to block your desire to communicate. Should you simply ask a question, your mate may react with a scornful look of disgust that sends the message:

- "I'm disgusted with who you are."
- "What's wrong with you?"
- "Are you stupid?"
- "Why would you ask that?"

And just like that, your question (an attempt at connection) has been blocked with a sneer. The conversation is over.

Blocking frequently becomes accusatory. Even as you process the reason why your question provoked a sneer, you find yourself on the defensive—because you had the audacity to ask a question. You might receive a response such as:

- "You think you know it all."
- "It is not always about you."
- "You cannot be trusted, so I don't tell you anything."
- "You always have to have the last word."

Each of these accusations is yet another projection. Your mate (who claims to knows it all, who makes it all about her, who cannot be trusted, and must have the final word) manipulates you through accusatory tactics—to believe she does not want to communicate because you are not trustworthy or because you have "offended" her—when you have said or done nothing to be offensive.

> **Any attempt to emotionally connect with a narcissistic individual will result in manipulation—because of her invulnerability and trauma. Should you not recognize the manipulation, you will get "sucked in" to the same circular arguments, time and time again.**

Despite your mate's significant lack of awareness, you have voluntarily chosen to engage in interpersonal discussions that require emotional intelligence—hoping that maybe this time, you might be heard and understood. Despite the fact that this *magical* moment has never happened, you keep hoping things will eventually "get better" and you can fix the relationship through your efforts to communicate, or get through to your mate.

This is the pleaser's control. Time after time, pleasers come into my office and insist that the problem is one of communication. While communication is an issue, they have no awareness of just how critical emotional intelligence is to the process of communication, listening, and comprehension. Pleasers do not understand just how deep the roots of their mate's trauma go—and that an emotionally invulnerable individual is simply incapable of interpersonal conversations that involve listening, sharing, comprehension, ownership, understanding, trust, and love. All of these involve some level of emotional awareness, self-worth, and some capacity to feel and process uncomfortable emotions.

Yet pleasers seem to insist their mate's pathology is not *that* bad—and prefer to remain in denial. The narcissist is not the only stubborn one with control issues in the abusive relationship. Pleasing is simply the other side of the same coin. Both the narcissist and the pleaser often have the same compulsion to live in some alternate reality. Until the pleaser can accept that he is actively participating in an abusive relationship with a pathological liar, and that he is lying to himself by conflating "quitting" with "letting go"—and "escaping" as "failure"—he continues to convince himself he will eventually be seen, heard, and understood by his manipulative mate. Both the pleaser and the narcissist attempt to bend reality in whatever direction their ego requires—and refuse to accept that the abusive insanity is caused by a lack of emotional awareness on both sides.

Both share deep insecurities, and—in many ways—the same willfulness to obey the wants of their egos at the expense of feeling their feelings and listening to themselves. In other words, both lack the ability to discern, decide, and trust themselves—because of deep emotional repression and trauma. Hence, both prefer to lie to themselves that their hellish reality can be salvaged—without having to end the hostile, dependent, and dangerous relationship. Because of deep attachment and abandonment issues, both go to great lengths—to rationalize the relationship is better than it is—if only the other would change just a little bit more. Desperate to avoid the pain of leaving, the pleaser once more attempts to convince his narcissistic mate (after thousands of unsuccessful attempts) that he did not do what she says he did, or did say what she says he did not say—as if this time will be the "magical" moment that she believes and trusts him.

Forgetting

Forgetting, like so many other forms of communication, is often not recognized to be manipulation. In your mate's flight from responsibility, she frequently forgets important things that you, or she, have previously said or done:

- "I don't remember saying that."
- "That did not happen."
- "You're making that up."
- "Don't lie to me."

Just like that (in the middle of what you thought was a simple conversation), your reality is once again denied. What actually happened, did not happen—because your mate "forgot" it actually happened. She feels no need to reflect to jog her memory. You are now left doubting yourself—about what you *know* actually happened ... and whether it happened.

Your mate may conveniently omit portions of actual circumstances for the purpose of making herself look good—and to demonize you. Truth is frequently taken out of context to make you appear malicious. You have probably noticed this pattern many times in your abusive relationship—and may not have even considered forgetting to be a form of manipulation. But now that you do, another piece of the puzzle falls into place.

It is my sincere hope that this chapter has been empowering (and eye-opening) towards assisting you to recognize the various forms of manipulation—for the purpose of learning to trust and validate your own perceptions, feelings, and experiences. In so doing, you will gradually release your need to please—and eventually come to care less about what your narcissistic mate thinks about you.

The fact of the matter is: *Your mate is not the person you thought she was.* With a new set of eyes, you can now see her to be the insecure, invulnerable, petulant child that she has always been—and know that she is incapable of changing inside your co-dependent relationship. Hopefully, you can now see that your narcissistic relationship has been nothing more than a one-directional, hypocritical lie—designed only to benefit your mate so she can steal your power and take full advantage of you whenever she can—all because she feels "ripped off" from a good life—and can now justify ripping you off from yours—so that she can steal as much of *you* as she can.

Are you ready to accept that you deserve more than you are receiving? Are you ready to choose to move forward and accept your narcissistic mate is never going to change? That she will never get better or stop abusing you inside your abusive relationship?

I truly hope that you can accept the reality of your abusive relationship—and the reality you must leave. The manipulation that you are absorbing every day is killing your psyche and robbing you of confidence and self-worth—one subtle, manipulative attack at a time.

WARNING: As you recognize the manipulation, consider your decision, subtlety disengage, and make little changes to yourself—be sure not to say a word to your mate. You should now be on the alert—that your mate may sniff out any changes you make. Things may quickly take a turn for the worse. **You will want to being making plans to leave without saying a word—and lawyer up immediately. Time may be of the essence.**

5

Implosion

Several years ago, I worked with a kind, likable and emotionally-available father—whose wife had recently imploded and made allegations to the police that he had physically assaulted her.

Two weeks earlier, Thomas, his wife Wendy, and their three children were eating supper at the dinner table. There was tension in the air—as there often was in the family home. Eventually, the eldest child, Sarah (10), broke the silence —and asked if she could invite a friend to her sister's birthday party the following afternoon.

Sarah's request was immediately squashed. "You don't need a friend at your sister's party," Wendy shot back, irritated by her daughter's question.

An explanation was not provided and Sarah's request was immediately denied. She froze—sitting quietly in her chair, as tears began rolling down her cheeks. More silence—as the tension around the table escalated. Empathizing with his daughter, and carefully calculating what he might say, Thomas decided to advocate on his daughter's behalf. "Why can't Sarah invite a friend, Wendy?"

"I don't need to give you a reason," Wendy fired back, offended that her husband would challenge her authority.

Moments passed in silence. Sarah stopped crying. Then Lacey, their eight-year-old middle child, broke the silence—attempting to lighten the mood. "Can we all go camping in a few weeks when the weather warms up?"

"No." Wendy closed her eyes and shook her head, as if she could not tolerate that the children might have wants and needs.

The other family members sat at the table, heads down, absorbing what was happening. Thomas felt bad for both of his daughters and responsible for protecting them. He again decided to break the silence. "Wendy, I can look into some campsites and see what's available," he said, hoping that Wendy might be agreeable to the needs of the children.

"I already said No!" Wendy was now angry that her husband was "undermining" her authority in front of the children. She then aggressively pushed her chair back, banged both hands on the table, and got up. Wendy ordered both girls to follow her, grabbed her infant Zachery, marched up to her room, and immediately phoned her sister, reporting, "Thomas is being a dick. He's such an asshole. I'm coming over with the kids."

Wendy hung up the phone and barked another order to her anxious children—who were now frozen with fear, "Come on. We're leaving."

Wendy marched back down the stairs, the children not saying a word—too terrified to challenge their mother. Wendy grabbed the keys to the car and proceeded to exit the house. Expecting that Wendy might leave with the children, Thomas was waiting at the door—hoping he could convince his wife to stay. This was not the first time Wendy had become unstable because Thomas questioned her authority. She had left with the children many times before—without telling Thomas what she was doing—or when she would be returning.

"You don't have to leave," Thomas implored. He was terrified. In the past, Wendy had left with the children for days—refusing to indicate where she was going, how long she would be gone, or even whether she would be returning. During these dramatic episodes, Thomas would be abandoned by his wife—and the children would be withheld to punish him—for having "caused" the most recent "conflict." Hoping to avoid this terror again, Thomas met Wendy at the door and desperately tried to convince her to stay.

"You don't need to leave Wendy. I have to go to work now anyways."

Wendy ordered her husband out of the way and continued to exit the house, now in a rage. Thomas's words were ignored, while the children looked to guidance from their frightened and helpless father.

Now desperate and terrified, Thomas assumed Wendy might just leave for good this time. His abandonment issues were now fully activated—as Wendy pushed past him at the door. Just as she did, Thomas grabbed the keys out of his wife's hand. No sooner had he done this, then he realized he had made a grave mistake.

"There," she said, nodding her head, and smiling smugly. "Now you've done it."

Wendy's rage had reached a crescendo—as she ordered the children to follow her back upstairs—and again phoned her sister. She said, "Thomas just grabbed me in front of the kids and shook me. He wouldn't let me go. I had to run up the stairs to get away from him. Phone the police."

Wendy's sister was now manipulated to believe her sibling was now in physical danger. Hence, she got off the phone and immediately phoned the police.

Having just lied to her sister, Wendy then yelled down the stairs, "The police are on their way."

Thomas was horrified, shocked, paralyzed, and confused—by how quickly this altercation at the door had escalated from dinner at the table to the police being called. Shocked and panicked—he could feel the energy leaving his body as terror mounted. All Thomas could do now was sit down on the bench in the front entrance—and wait for the police to arrive. Thoughts raced through his mind: *What's going to happen now? I cannot believe this is happening. She's never called the police before. What is she going to tell them? Who are the police going to believe? This isn't going to end well.*

Sitting on the bench, his children upstairs, having been ordered to stay with their mother against their will, all Thomas could do was wait—as an aching feeling of dread welled up inside. He knew nothing he could say to Wendy would make a damn bit of difference at this point. Her mind would be made up.

He couldn't help but think to himself: *Who are the police going to believe in a domestic incident? This will be a case of she said, he said. There will be no going back from here.*

While Thomas sat on the bench—waiting for police to arrive—he knew Wendy was about to manipulate the police to see her as the "victim" in a domestic disturbance. He knew full well what his wife was capable of. All Thomas could do was wait in the front entrance—and prepare himself for what was likely to be a very bad situation.

Several minutes passed and suddenly, there was a knock on the door.

Thomas got up from his bench, opened the door, and greeted both officers standing on his front step. "We're responding to a domestic violence call. Can we come in?"

The officers entered and asked where Wendy was located. Then, one of them proceeded up the stairs to interview Wendy, while the second officer remained with Thomas. The children were sent downstairs to wait with their father, while Wendy was interviewed privately. After about thirty minutes, the officer came down to speak to (not interview) Thomas. "I'm informing you that allegations of physical assault have been made against you. Under the circumstances, you'll be required to leave your property and come with us to ensure everyone's safety."

Without being interviewed or provided an opportunity to give his perception of events, Thomas was asked to turn around and face the wall—at which point he was handcuffed in front of his children—and escorted from his home to a squad car sitting out front. Once inside the vehicle (and still handcuffed), Thomas attempted to explain his version of events—noticing neither officer seemed overly interested—nor were they taking notes.

Thomas was informed he was being charged with physical assault—and would require a criminal lawyer. Feeling powerless, shocked, and terrified, he quietly attempted to come to terms with the insane turn of events that had just transpired. New thoughts were racing through his mind: *My relationship is over. I have no idea when I'm going to get to see my children again. I'm actually being charged with assault! Could I really go to jail for this? If I go to jail, I could lose my job, my house, my kids—everything!*

Flash forward a couple of weeks and here he was—sitting in my office, recalling the abuse that had led him to reach out for help. Still coming to terms with the recent fall-out, and crisis in his life, Thomas would now begin the painful, psychological process of picking up the pieces of his shattered life—which had been the culmination of twelve years of pleasing, avoiding conflict, morphing himself, and emotional and physical abuse.

Obviously, the incident with the police had been a slow boil—leading to an implosion of anger, hate, and punishment. Yet, the reality had been that Wendy and Thomas had been desperately trying to change one other—through control and submission for 12 years—and neither accepted the destructive reality of their toxic relationship.

In the two weeks since the implosion, Thomas had not been permitted to see his three children, Lacey (10), Sarah (6), and Zackery (18 months). Wendy had obtained a No Contact Order the day following the incident. Now living with his parents, Thomas had retained a family lawyer to obtain shared custody of his children—and a criminal lawyer to defend against the charges of physical assault. His family lawyer had just recently obtained weekend visitation rights with the children. Thomas's parents would be permitted to pick the children up in the next couple of days.

This had been the implosion and the early stages of the fall out—just after a chaotic incident erupted out of nothing—that led to Thomas's arrest and removal from his home.

In a power struggle of control (that constitutes an abusive relationship), both the narcissist and the pleaser stubbornly refuse to interrupt the trauma bond, confront their subsequent dependency issues—or let go of their deep need to change the perceptions, reality, and behavior of the other.

The implosion is the culmination of abuse (including the pleaser's toleration and participation in it) that invariably erupts at some point in an abusive relationship. In their battle to secure love from the other, both the narcissist and pleaser stubbornly refuse to let go of their trauma bond and confront their dependency issues. In other words, both actively trivialize their own behavior and refuse to face the only sane choice before them. Instead, they attempt to change each other (which is nothing short of a pathological power struggle.)

Having met twelve years earlier, Thomas now informed me that the couple had never got along, but chose to "try and make things work" because of an unplanned pregnancy and religious beliefs.

Like many abusive relationships, the couple had become pregnant early in the relationship. At that point, Wendy's control and manipulation ramped up. She also knew Thomas would be a dedicated, emotionally-available father—even before the baby was born. Wendy knew she could use the unborn baby as a "pawn"—to ensure submission, should Thomas not do precisely what he was told.

Threats, followed by accusations, were introduced at this transitional stage of the relationship. Thomas had become exhausted from pleasing—and could no longer meet Wendy's endless expectations and needs. He would be accused of being "uncaring," "selfish," and even "abusive" towards her. Of course, these threats and accusations invoked terror in Thomas—as he felt that Wendy would definitely abandon him (with his child) if he did not do exactly as she demanded.

As Wendy had predicted, when their first child, Sarah, was born, Thomas dove into his new role as a father—while at the same time, Her expectations and abuse ramped up. Still confused and hoping the abuse would not be permanent, Thomas decided marriage would be a good decision—even though the red flags were flying high. But Thomas's fear of abandonment—and the possibility Wendy would withhold his baby should she leave, kept him doing what he knew how to do—bend over backwards and convince himself he was doing the "right" thing.

Like so many men in abusive relationships, Thomas rationalized he could win Wendy over—by accepting all responsibility for the abuse—and by continuing to morph himself into whomever she needed him to be. If he could just explain himself better, justify his actions, and try a little harder, he would prove himself to be a dependable and trustworthy partner. Certainly then, Wendy would be satisfied with his efforts—and return his love.

Intuitively, Thomas suspected he should be leaving, but lacked the ability to trust himself. He did not believe he deserved to be treated better, nor was he prepared to legally stand up to Wendy—to obtain shared custody. Hence, he trivialized his abuse and hoped he could make his wife happy. In so doing, Thomas rationalized he could avoid the pain of separation and the inevitable custody battle.

This process of "becoming better" (on the part of the pleaser) is not motivated by a desire to improve oneself, but simply to gain approval. Hence, pleasing is not authentic personality change—but simply manipulation through accommodation. In the pleaser's desperate attempt to gain favor with his wife, he gives himself away—piece by piece—until he has lost himself.

> All pleasers appease their narcissistic girlfriend or wife through accommodation. They are not being true to themselves—nor are they being honest with their mate. This is their control and manipulation. Once pleasers become aware that something is wrong in their toxic relationship, they still rationalize that they can fix the relationship—without any participation from their mate.

In Thomas's case, the children, too, were being abused. At one point, Wendy killed Sarah's pet guinea pig—because she was "sick of the smell in the house." When her daughter returned home from school, Wendy justified her actions—without an ounce of empathy—telling Sarah, "We don't have enough money for pet food." Shocked, horrified, and traumatized, Sarah could not believe what her mother had done—and would now have to grieve the loss of her pet.

Another incident involved Wendy dragging Sarah down two flights of stairs—one hand behind her neck and the other over her mouth—to stop her daughter from screaming. Red marks on Sarah's neck bore evidence of the physical abuse. But Thomas did not report the incident to Social Services, nor did he attempt to charge his wife. This would mean standing up to Wendy, potentially gaining full custody of the children, and making the critical decision to leave. Instead, he felt sorry for Wendy, and hoped he could gain favor by enabling her.

> So often, pleasers feel sorry for their abusive mates—and enable the abuse—even when they have opportunities and choices before them—to stop the abuse and protect themselves and their children.

During this first session, Thomas unpacked (for the first time), some of the emotional and physical abuse he and his children had been experiencing for many years—that had culminated into the recent implosion. Now sitting in my office, he seemed to feel some reprieve—having finally told someone about the nightmare he had been living with for over a decade.

Thomas believed that his world was now shattered—and seemed to see darkness in every direction. It was then that I took the opportunity to reframe the experience for Thomas. "Have you ever considered that this crisis is an opportunity or blessing in disguise? Should this implosion not have happened, you would still be tolerating and allowing your abuse to continue—and that of your children's. You can now use this opportunity to gain shared custody of your children and give them a life free of abuse and a fully dedicated father—at least half of the time."

Thomas replied, "I had never looked at it that way."

During our second session, Thomas informed me that Wendy had been texting him—despite the No Contact Order she had instigated. He confirmed he would be informing his lawyer that Wendy was breaching the No Contact Order. He read me one of the texts: *I really miss you. I hope you can come home soon.* Even though Wendy had recently made allegations of assault—and then requested a No Contact Order, she was now wanting her husband to return home after the Order expired. Should Thomas have made the mistake of responding to Wendy's text (in which he was tempted to do), he could have been charged for violating the Order.

Fortunately, Thomas resisted the temptation to return Wendy's texts (thanks in part to the No Contact Order). The Order, and the threat of further violations, were forcing Thomas to disengage, hold boundaries, and continue to let go. This would mark the first time he had never responded to Wendy (disengaged) when she had reached out. These external forces—initially designed to punish him—were now actually helping Thomas stay away and detach. He would not previously have had the strength to do this. Without legal implications, Thomas may have responded to his wife's texts, in the hope that they could reunite and work things out.

From a therapeutic perspective, Thomas was moving in the right direction. The trauma bond (which is nothing short of an addiction) needed to be broken—and ironically the legal system was assisting him with this process.

Thomas had also been granted visitation rights and was now about to see his children every weekend—another victory towards increased access to his children. He had now created the opportunity to parent his children on his terms—free of control. Yet no sooner had he obtained visitation rights, than the children began disclosing that their mother was telling (manipulating) them, "Mommy says that you're gay. She told us to watch you when you change Zackery's diaper, so you do not play with his private parts."

Manipulation of the children by the narcissistic parent against the emotionally available parent—during and after the fall-out phase—is common. Therefore, it is suggested you document all abusive incidents and present them to your lawyer.

Like most narcissists at separation, Wendy had entered a pathological state of grieving—in which she had become even more hateful, angry, malicious, and vengeful. Typically narcissists do not experience sadness or depressive states at separation. Instead, they tend to hate their partner for "abandoning" them, a crime they had no "right" to commit. The narcissistic now experiences overwhelming feelings of hatred, betrayal, and revenge—resulting from the massive loss of control they no longer have over their ex-partner.

In her pathological state of grieving, Wendy had begun manipulating her children against their father—in an insidious attempt to gain the approval of her children and punish their father. Unlike Thomas, Wendy had not developed a strong emotional attachment with her children, and frequently been jealous of them for the love they showed their father. Because the children had a much stronger emotional attachment to their father, they trusted him—and were now disclosing what their mother was telling them on their most recent visit.

Hence, the manipulation was not having the desired effect. In fact, the children were actually fighting back—by disclosing what their mother was saying to them. Sarah disclosed, "Mommy says you drink too much and watch porn."

In her pathological state of grieving, Wendy needed the children to side with her—as allies against their father whom they trusted and loved.

If she could turn the children against their father, Wendy could both steal their love and punish Thomas for daring to stand up for himself, seek shared custody, and free himself from the chains of her control. According to Wendy, Thomas did not deserve his children because he abandoned her—even though it was Wendy who abandoned him.

Even though Thomas knew the type of cruelty Wendy was capable of, he could not comprehend why she would abuse the children—just to punish him. He shared some of his thoughts: *She's hates me so much that she's damaging the children to punish me? What if the Courts ultimately believe her? Where the hell does she come up with this crap? I'm a pedophile now? I'm gay? I'm an alcoholic?*

Thomas continued to be shocked, tormented and terrified—as we continued to work through his feelings and experiences. Forcing himself forward, Thomas was attempting to make sense of Wendy's campaign of revenge—as he stood his ground—and believed in himself for the first time in his life.

Unfortunately, the manipulation of the children was affecting Sarah's mental health. She was now having panic attacks at school—and self-harming at her mother's. She would continue to disclose to her father what her mother was saying to her. "Daddy does not know how to love." "I don't want your dad washing your hair. He might play with your private parts."

I had already reported the psychological abuse of the children to Social Services—as did Thomas and the school counsellor.

Thomas was trying to help his children in any way possible, including hiring a tutor for Sarah to support her falling grades. But Wendy would actively sabotage his efforts—jealous that her children loved their father. She could see her children pulling away and resented them for it. Children were supposed to be "seen" and not "heard.' The children's love for their father—and their perceived rejection of her enraged Wendy even more.

Feeling a tremendous loss of control over her husband and children, Wendy's behavior had become highly erratic and unstable. One evening, while Sarah was on the phone with her tutor, Wendy stormed into the living room and ripped the phone out of her daughter's hand. She proceeded to attack the tutor, stating, "We don't need your help anymore!" and slammed down the phone. Sarah erupted into tears because of the aggressive behavior of her mother. Wendy countered, "Stop being a baby. You don't need a tutor."

Wendy hated that Thomas had access to the children and that he was actually supporting them. This meant he was gaining power—and independently making choices in the best interests of the children—something he would not have been permitted to do when he lived with her. This meant that Wendy no longer ruled unilaterally over the children. This loss of control only infuriated her further.

Apparently, Thomas was supposed to lie down and die—except that he was not. He was doing quite the opposite. Thomas had retained two lawyers, obtained visitation rights on the weekends, entered therapy, and reported the psychological and physical abuse of the children to both the police and Social Services. Despite having thrown everything she could at Thomas, he was bouncing back—and no longer submitting. Instead, he was now standing up for himself, supporting his children, and ignoring Wendy. He was even hoping to gain full custody of the children because of their mother's abuse towards them.

During our third session, Thomas informed me that he was missing Wendy. Despite the fact she was trying to destroy him—and damaging the mental health of their children, he too was grieving. Thomas still felt love towards Wendy and hoped she might come to see what she was doing—and take responsibility for her abusive behavior. Thomas had not yet accepted the deep pathology of his wife and the fact and that this was never going to happen.

> Despite the ongoing, repetitive, and consistent abuse they experience, most men still love their narcissistic girlfriend or wife. Because of the love they feel—as well as being deeply entrenched in the grieving process—many entertain the notion of returning to their mate.

This is what the fall-out phase in an abusive relationship often looks like. Thomas still loved Wendy. It was a toxic kind of love—but the only type of love he knew. Hence, working through the grieving process was extremely painful for Thomas—as he quietly nursed hopes that Wendy would see the error of her ways. This is what a trauma bond looks and feels like. Despite the insidious abuse, partners still love their mates— and still cling to hope. Thomas was now experiencing the legitimate pain of grief and letting go—the very pain he had been avoiding for twelve years.

> Most pleasers (in their insecure attachment), would rather tolerate the abuse—than experience the pain of grief. It is this grief process that so many attempt to avoid—and one of the main reasons pleasers often stay.

Escape often means experiencing this painful grieving process—while at the same time, dealing with ongoing abuse and a legal process. Many feel that they are not strong enough to cope with these painful emotional pressures and the grief involved. At the core of these painful dynamics is low self-worth. For both the pleaser and the narcissist, the grieving process can be extremely painful—as each inwardly blames themselves to have been "failures" because the relationship did not work. A pleaser often believes he deserves no better treatment that what he is receiving.

Fortunately, at the fall-out phase, the pleaser is forced to undergo the legitimate suffering of grief in which he *must* successfully get through— by battling his many temptations to go back. The grieving process is a significant factor in severing the trauma bond. The pleaser must learn to discipline himself—and say "No" to himself. He must learn to make difficult decisions—based on what is right and responsible—as opposed to simply submitting to the will of his desires. He must battle his hope that the relationship can be salvaged.

As we began our fourth session together, Thomas was romanticizing the good times in the relationship and grieving Wendy's loss. He began the session by saying, "I don't know what I want sometimes. I miss my house. I miss my old life. I miss our lifestyle—and I miss Wendy. I still sometimes think we could make it work."

This was the real challenge for Thomas—making it through the grieving process that ultimately requires discernment, discipline, dedication to reality, commitment, and perseverance. This process involved learning to discipline himself—to battle his own impulses to return to Wendy by rationalizing that he could make things work. This is where pleasers tend to get "stuck"—in the self-deception that they can bend reality to the will of their desires—as opposed to choosing, feeling, and experiencing the necessary and healthy process of grief. For Thomas, the No Contact Order assisted the grieving process—by forcing him to stay away from Wendy when left to his own devices, he may not have.

I reminded Thomas that making the decision at some point to go back—by submitting to the pain of his necessary grieving process, would be the same as abandoning himself—and his children's mental health, for the purpose of ending the legitimate suffering of grief. Grieving *is* a required process of letting go, developing confidence, and releasing the need for external approval.

Deep down, Thomas knew what I was saying was true, but he required the push and the validation I was providing to keep him moving forward—and to keep him from relapsing. He was beginning to discern what the right decisions were moving forward and battling against his compulsion to submit to his grief and go back.

> **This process of discernment, self-control, and perseverance (as opposed to giving in to your impulse to assuage your pain) is critical to persevering through the grieving process.**

A few days later, Thomas received a huge break. His perseverance would ultimately tip the scales of his legal case—and provide more validation he was making the right decision. While the police had been reviewing video-taped testimony by Wendy for the upcoming Court proceedings, an officer noticed she was smirking during the interview—proving she had been lying during her testimony. The charges were immediately dropped.

Events were turning Thomas's way. No longer would he require a criminal lawyer. No longer would he worry about going to jail, losing his job, or infinitely worse—his children. From this turn of good fortune, Thomas would now obtain shared custody of his children and actively parent them—free from Wendy's abuse—for the first time in his family's history.

All Thomas's efforts were paying off. He was learning to stand up for himself, trust himself, grieve, and release his insecure attachment of pleasing. He had made it through the worst of the fall-out and would receive shared custody of his children. Thomas was free from his abuse.

Had Thomas not been escorted out of his own home—against his will—he would have continued to actively participate in the trauma bond he and Wendy had created.

The implosion had simply been the inevitable consequence of massive control on both sides. Both refused to end the toxic nightmare because of their own *willfulness*. Both believed they could change the other through coercive manipulation.

> **Pretending to be someone you are not—to get love and approval—
> has never worked for anyone, at any time—and never will.**

Until such time an abused man is *ready* to escape, he remains a prisoner (both to the abuse and to the will of his own egoic wants and needs). He ignores patterns, remains indecisive, and refuses to learn from his mistakes—all while deceiving himself into believing he is better off remaining in the status quo of his abusive relationship—instead of learning from his mistakes and committing himself to reality. Without the development of self-esteem—integrity, trust, reason, and self-respect—are essentially non-existent. Unless or until, the pleaser is ready to go through the grieving process, he is not likely to develop the above attributes of self-esteem.

> **Is it time to get real with yourself? Can you accept that the chains
> of your trauma bond must be broken? Is it time to acknowledge that
> you and your children are *not* better off in an abusive relationship?
> Can you admit that you have been deceiving yourself?**

It is not as if Thomas's children were protected from Wendy's mental or physical abuse—or somehow better off because he chose to stay for twelve years. Clearly they were not! Keeping the family together was obviously not the healthy, responsible, or functional decision for anyone involved. There was no virtue in Thomas's "commitment" to Wendy—that he had made twelve years earlier.

Thomas was just one of a vast number of men forced out of their abusive relationships by implosion—when their narcissistic wife literally lost control. The obvious lesson inherent in an abusive relationship is this: *You must, at some point, decide to stand up to the bully—who just happens to be your girlfriend or wife. You must become ready to willingly choose the legitimate suffering of grief, change, fall-out, and separation—by experiencing and persevering through the pain—no matter how terrified you are. By doing this painful work, you will learn to trust yourself, develop self-esteem, and free yourself from the chains of abuse—and pleasing. It is in this way (through this painful process), that individuals learn to trust and respect themselves, release their need to please, and protect their children in the process.*

Thomas's wake-up call was (like so many others) indeed, *a gift*. The choice was literally made for him (out of hate, jealousy, and feelings of betrayal). From his wife's loss of control and ultimate implosion, his journey into freedom, personal responsibility, and true power arose!

Unless or until you make the only responsible and healthy choice to escape, you will decay and continue to devolve into anxiety, confusion, and defeat—as you hide from what you know deep down to be the truth—that you must escape the terrorist that you love.

> **This book is designed to kick men in the ass, wake them up, and push them forward—into an amazing life for themselves and their children.**

This new reality is more than possible—should you heed the wake-up call! We have all heard the phrase: The definition of insanity is choosing to do the same thing over and over again—expecting a different result. Choosing to remain in a narcissistic relationship is the definition of insanity. It *is* literally making the same, insane decision to stay—at the cost of your mental health and that of your children's.

Several years after I worked with Thomas, we recently went out to dinner to catch up. He is now happy and remarried, both of his daughters live with him full-time—having made this choice as soon as they were of age. He enjoys a satisfying relationship with both of his girls—and his son who lives with him half-time.

For those of you in a narcissistic relationship, hopefully you can see there is definitely real hope—that you can choose to reclaim your personal power—and create a far better life for yourself and your children. You are not "stuck" or "chained" in an abusive relationship. You can break your own chains of pleasing—and you can certainly break your mate's chains of control.

The fact that Thomas obtained half-time custody (and eventually full custody) of his children gave them the shot they needed to have a healthy life—eventually free of their mother's abuse. They just needed one healthy, emotionally-available home—to recover from the abuse they received at the hands of their mother. Had Thomas not escaped, his children might well have become statistics.

The ultimate result of his escape—was his own mental health and that of his children's. The implosion and escape made all the difference in the world. Ultimately, a child's emotions need to be validated—if they are to develop the ability to trust themselves. When this happens, the children are no longer as vulnerable to the manipulation and power plays of others—and they learn to respect and trust themselves. Hence, the likelihood they attract or tolerate narcissistic individuals is significantly diminished.

Once the implosion occurred, Thomas was ultimately victorious in reclaiming his power and saving his children from full-time abuse. In the end, his wake-up call was the blessing it was designed to be. In a very real way, Thomas saved himself and his children from a steady decline into feelings of worthlessness and self-loathing.

> The inherent message throughout the book is: Do not wait for implosion. You now know that it is inevitable. Become ready and face the pain that you fear—and reclaim your happiness and freedom in the process.

The reality is—huge numbers of men around the globe feel trapped in narcissistic relationships. This is not a secret. Men must summon the courage to face their fears and doubts, uproot insecurities, and trust they will be successful in getting their children half-time. Don't underestimate the power that resides within you.

6

Out of Ego, Dependency, and Low Self-Esteem

It is all about her. It always has been. It always will be. Your mate cares only about stealing your love through manipulative means. And you care only about getting her love—by appeasing and compromising yourself. This too is manipulative.

Remember the steady feeding of love and attention your mate required—right from the get go. Your attachment (trauma bond) happened quickly. To obtain the care and attention she required, your mate controlled you through manipulative means—and you would allow it—careful not to lose her.

Your girlfriend was needy and dependent—yes. But were you aware of your own dependency issues? Why would you have tolerated control and manipulation if you were not desperate and dependent yourself? Prior to meeting, you both felt lonely and desperate for love. For you, your loneliness ended when you both met. Your lover had finally arrived.

You may have been mesmerized by her physical beauty. Hence, you probably put her on a pedestal.

Having an attractive woman in your life made you feel better about yourself—and provided an external sense of self-worth.

The fact that your girlfriend was interested in you felt exciting (like an emotional high) just as your interest, attention, care, and adoration felt exciting to her—and made her feel better about herself. Back in those days, it was all good—so long as you were together—so long as you were stroking each other's ego.

Eventually you were forced to pull back and recharge, but this was tricky business. You certainly did not want to lose your new girlfriend. It was not as if you felt the relationship would have to end, you just needed a break—but didn't have a clue what you were up against. As a pleaser, you did not care enough about your own needs and feelings to confront your mate. Hence, you continued to compromise yourself without realizing you were stretching yourself thin—and as you did, you were deceiving your mate to think this was who you truly were.

Unfortunately, it was not long before your tank was low—and the light was on "E." Keeping your girlfriend happy and satisfied was proving to be more than you bargained for. But what choice did you have? You would have to keep her happy—or risk confusing conversations that would never end. Neither of these were good options, right? But damn—your mate's neediness, clinginess, control, and manipulation were pushing you to the edge—of losing yourself.

Until this point in the relationship, you had tolerated the one-sided conversations that had come to define your relationship. You had abandoned yourself through avoidance—by not telling your mate how her behavior was making your feel. This would be too much of a risk. Yet, something now had to be said. You were beyond exhausted—and the feeding frenzy needed to stop! It was time to have that difficult talk. You had nothing more to give? You braced yourself for a discussion that may have gone like this: "Can we talk for a for a few minutes? It is kind of important. Lately I've been feeling pretty overwhelmed. I need to take a little more time to myself. I love spending time with you, but I'm having a tough time staying on top of things."

Hoping your mate would understand and be okay with you taking a little more time to yourself (without having to address her needy, controlling, and manipulative behavior) may have been how you broached the issue—hoping not to offend her. Finally, you had mustered up the courage to say at least some of what you needed to say, but were hoping for a better reaction than the one you received: "Why wouldn't you want to be with me? I don't understand why spending time with me is so difficult for you? Why would you want to deprive me of love? I feel like you're being selfish."

Just like that, your words were twisted back around to somehow be your fault. It was you who was now accused of being selfish—because you wanted some time to yourself—to maintain some balance in your life. Soon, this pattern of manipulation had become the norm. Yet, you would not have recognized the manipulation, nor would you have had the words to describe what you were experiencing.

You would not have known what you were dealing with, nor would you have known that manipulation was a permanent characteristic of your mate's narcissistic personality disorder. Hence, you continued to show your mate that you really did care about her—and were not being selfish. You then compromised yourself, did what she wanted, and swept your needs under the carpet. The mere thought of the relationship ending—and going back to loneliness and feelings of worthlessness was worse (in your mind) than the confusing reality you were experiencing at the time.

Had you continued the above conversation—hoping to get your girlfriend to understand you needed some time to yourself—and that this did not mean you did not enjoy spending time with her, by saying, "I'm starting to feel like whatever I want does not matter. Whenever I try and talk about how I feel—it gets twisted back onto me."

No sooner had you uttered these words (and precisely to your point), the finger was pointed back at you: "Why would you not want to be with me? Why would you ever want to say 'No' to me? I don't understand why spending time with me is so hard for you?"

Without knowing who, or what, you were dealing with—you were sucked back into another circular discussion that went nowhere: "That's not what I meant. That's not what I said."

Eventually, you learned that expressing your feelings, wants, and needs—was not going to be possible in your romantic relationship. At the same time, you would not have understood the real danger of who and what you were dealing with—a narcissistic love partner. You would not have understood why you were never heard—why you were never understood—or why you may have been accused of cheating—or some other malicious behavior. Hence, you kept second-guessing yourself—and later convincing yourself that you would eventually find a way to get through to your mate who (for some reason) just never seemed to get you.

In the previous chapter, we looked at the implosion of a 12-year cycle of dependency and abuse. In this chapter, we will look at how trauma bonds and dependency issues are formed and strengthened.

In abusive relationships, neither the pleaser nor the narcissist have any idea of what constitutes a healthy, loving relationship—having never been exposed to one. Real love is free of convincing, proving, earning, manipulation, and control of any kind. Such relationships permit and promote individuality, autonomy, and equality.

Autonomy is not permitted in abusive relationships. Both the narcissist and the pleaser need the approval, validation, and love of the other—as neither knows what constitutes a healthy, romantic relationship. Each set about winning over, impressing, convincing, locking down, helping and proving themselves—to get the love of the other. Love is no more than a subjective feeling that stems from ego attachment—which is often based (and strengthened) from the physical aspect of the relationship. Because each feel undeserving of the other, both put their best foot forward to gain the love and admiration of the other.

In healthy romantic relationships (where real love, honesty, and boundaries exist), both individuals choose their freedom—and trust themselves to make their own autonomous decisions—while respecting their partner to do the same. Controlling or changing one another is not something either desires to do. Each have the awareness to process, regulate, and accept responsibility for their own feelings, behavior, and decisions—and the courage to openly express themselves. Neither seek the validation of the other—knowing that happiness and fulfillment originate from within.

In dependent, abusive relationships, this level of emotional intelligence and self-esteem does not exist. Both the pleaser and the narcissist choose the security of the relationship, and each need the positive regard of the other. Neither remain true to themselves, nor have they begun to work on themselves—learning what it means to like, respect, and trust themselves.

Because neither like, trust, or respect themself, each require the attention, love, and approval from the other—in order to feel better about themselves. Hence, honest communication does not occur. Moreover, the pleaser lacks the ability to set—and more importantly, hold boundaries—while boundaries (to the narcissist) mean absolutely nothing. Individuals who care about themselves express their feelings and needs—and then make decisions based on whether their feelings and needs are heard and respected. They are willing to end the relationship if their partner is not willing to respect them.

In dependent relationships, neither the narcissist nor the pleaser feel secure enough to be on their own. They have not begun the process of personal growth and, as a result, require the approval and attention of their mate to feel secure within themselves—and within the relationship. Neither knows what it means to be true to themselves— let alone partake in an honest conversation to repair conflict. Both remain terrified of potential rejection.

The pleaser will often not face his terror of abandonment—by discerning whether he should be getting out of the controlling, abusive relationship—until much further down the road—if he ever does at all. At this point in the pleaser's psychological development, his need for external validation is much stronger than his need for integrity, peace, freedom, and fulfillment.

Both the narcissist and the pleaser blame their actions (and reactions) to be the fault of the other, who is failing to love them as they need to be loved. Yet neither will terminate the relationship because of the grief and changes each feel powerless to deal with—nor can they trust themselves to make such a monumental decision. Terror of devastation—and fears of loss create doubt that the grass might not be greener on the other side.

Obviously, this is not real love. This is dependency. Both the pleaser and narcissist are highly dependent personalities, with insecure attachment issues. Genuine apologies, independent decisions, corrective actions, and the ability to process, repair, and resolve conflict are not possible within the abusive relationship. Both lack the self-awareness of their own missing pieces.

The narcissist gets love by controlling and manipulating the pleaser's perceptions, emotions, and behavior—in order to soothe her insecurities, while the pleaser gets love by regulating and controlling the narcissist's perceptions, emotions, and behavior—to soothe his insecurities. The narcissist attempts to convince the pleaser she has the right to be loved precisely how she demands to be loved—yet all the while she makes ludicrous accusations against him. He in turn, accommodates her paranoid accusations—in an attempt to regain her trust.

Neither can independently trust their own perceptions and feelings—without the validation of the other. Should the pleaser have a difference of opinion, the narcissist must convince him he is wrong. When such an attack is launched, the pleaser must then convince her that she is wrong about him—that he has not cheated or done what he has been accused of. Each are dependent on obtaining agreement and validation from the other.

Since the pleaser does not have the self-esteem to set or hold boundaries, morphing and submission become the norm—all while he struggles with both the recognition of the manipulation and awareness that his mate's disorder is permanent.

Often, separation is not an option because of the pleaser's abandonment issues. Confronting these issues involves the ability to make sacrifices and engage in the grieving process. For many, this loss of security and potential grief is more unattractive than the toleration of toxicity, anger, betrayal, and stagnation. The security of the abusive relationship is preferable to the sacrifices, losses, and grief involved—towards the development of self-esteem and confronting dependency issues.

Both the narcissist and pleaser are highly dependent on the other to make them feel better about themselves—and to provide internal security.

For the pleaser, the fear of abandonment, rejection, and separation is so great, he attempts to soothe his inner terror by convincing himself his narcissistic mate will one day see her behavior—and treat him better when she does. By clinging to this illusion, he believes he will not have to endure the pain of separation and face his pain of letting go. Hence, he will not have to exercise the courage to confront his abandonment issues and leave his abusive mate.

In making this highly irrational decision, the pleaser avoids putting energy into himself, learning what he is up against, getting honest with himself, and soothing his anxiety about making such a decision. Instead, he sweeps things under the carpet—or allows himself to get "sucked" back into yet another talk.

For your narcissistic mate, "talking" is code for control and manipulation. Her intension is always to crush you back into submission. To accomplish this, she must change your perceptions of reality to match her own. Then, when you have submitted (and compromised yourself once again in order to end the pain), the narcissist feels validated, emotionally secure, and back in control—at least for the moment.

These talks began early in your relationship—when you were busy convincing your mate of just how healthy, well-adjusted, and helpful you were. Because you lacked self-worth, and put her on a pedestal, you hid behind your mask—acting as if you were a healthy, caring love partner, willing to go to the ends of the earth for her. If you could impress your mate, worship her, and convince her that you were a great catch, you could "make" her love you.

Does this sound like you were being your authentic self? Of course not! You were morphing yourself into whomever you thought she wanted you to be—to win her love. Impressing your queen made you feel better about yourself. Meeting each and every one of her needs made you feel worthy and secure within the relationship. You could now show her how good you were—by meeting every one of her needs. Each time you succeed in making her happy, your new girlfriend would be grateful for the love, care, and support you provided. Then when she was pleased with you, you would feel secure within the relationship.

You may have noticed your mate became moody, depressed, and more cynical as time went on. Hence, you would "swoop" in and do your job of cheering her up, pampering her, and even babying her. Back in those days, so long as you were doing everything for her, you mate might permit you to see her emptiness or depressive episodes. Pampering, praising, listening, baths, massages, and constant reassurance you would never leave her seemed to do the job—at least for the moment.

Unfortunately for you, your mate's underlying depression, moodiness, and frequent need for reassurance made it impossible for you to successfully fulfill your job. Your tank was empty and someone—or something—had to give.

It may have been at this time in your relationship that your mate's behavior took a sharp turn for the worse. Even though you had attempted to share your feelings of exhaustion—your mate had not heard you. She was not about to let you take care of yourself—and take your power (autonomy) back.

Exhausted, you may have decided to express your needs once again. Continued submission and personal compromise was no longer an option. You may have mustered the courage up for another talk: "I'm still feeling pretty exhausted these days. I'm going to need a little more time to myself. I'm starting to feel like I cannot be me in this relationship."

"This wasn't part of our agreement," your girlfriend may have shot back. "This isn't fair. You're lucky to have me. You don't deserve me. This is why I agreed to date you. Because you were willing to take care of me."

Should you have heard some arrogant or entitled rant such as this, you may have thought to yourself: *Did she just imply I should be grateful to have her because she's so beautiful? That I had no right to take care of myself because I don't deserve her? That I should be happy with this one-directional relationship because I am not worthy of her?*

Arrogant rants like these may have been the first real glimpse into your girlfriend's entitled mind. You may have struggled to comprehend the words you were hearing at the time—that implied you did not share the same rights she did—or deserved to be treated in the same manner—because your status in the relationship was less than hers. Out of the horse's mouth, your girlfriend may have just told you that she had the right to get, take, and steal your attention, care, love, and autonomy—by any means necessary, while justifying she was better than you.

If you hadn't already figured out what you were dealing with, you may have been shocked by what you were hearing. Your job description had now been officially spelled out (in no uncertain terms) which meant you would now be dealing with yet another problem. Each time you exercised your own will, or had your own needs, you would be demeaned to be somehow undeserving of your mate. You may have thought to yourself: *What the hell is going on? Her responses don't even make sense! I'm not even sure I can fathom this level of arrogance. Is she for real? What crazy, upside-down universe have I landed in?*

You had just experienced a glimpse into your girlfriend's ego and entitlement. She had revealed her entitled self. While you may have experienced her needfulness and depressive episodes, until now, you may not have witnessed this level of arrogance and entitlement.

Had you respected yourself, you probably would have run for the hills. But you were insecurely attached—and had fallen for her. Perhaps, the physical aspect of the relationship felt addictive—or you convinced yourself you could never attract a woman of this physical caliber again. Feeling unworthy of your girlfriend, you probably ignored many red flags such as these—and rationalized you would eventually convince her you had needs of your own. Just give it time.

It is important to recognize the power of the physical and sexual aspects of the relationship—and how these dynamics cement ego attachments. The fact that your mate was attracted to you felt like "proof" you were desirable and loveable. Her interest in you definitely fed your ego.

Up to this point, sex may have been the basis of the relationship. Having a beautiful woman on your arm made you feel better about yourself, despite the fact she was robbing you of time and precious energy. While life may have been increasingly bizarre and dramatic, losing your mate was still not an option. You knew you would blame yourself for having "failed" at yet another romantic relationship—and attracting another woman of this physical caliber may not be possible again.

These dynamics explain why, in part, pleasers tolerate the abuse they receive. The powerful feeling of being wanted and chosen—along with the hope they will eventually obtain more of the love they so desperately desire—feels preferable to feeling lonely, empty, grieving, self-loathing, and blaming themselves should they make the decision to leave. Feelings of being wanted, desired, and chosen are powerful internal forces to contend with. Hoping to regain his previous feelings of being wanted again, the pleaser continues to go about accommodating his mate's false perceptions of him by doing whatever she wants of him. He hopes to regain these feelings of being wanted, desired, and attractive—and to regain some semblance of value.

Making the responsible decision to leave requires courage, self-awareness, and dedication to reality. The pleaser must make the courageous decision to see the writing on the wall for what it is—and not what he hopes it can be—if he is to arrive at the responsible, functional, and healthy decision to accept there will never be a way to be seen, heard, and respected by his narcissistic mate.

Going backwards to some previous time where your mate loved you and wanted you is never going to happen. The story you tell yourself about returning to a better past is nothing but an illusion. You must remind yourself of this—if you are going to push forward with disengagement and detachment.

In order to confront these deep abandonment issues, the pleaser must learn to release his fears, negative beliefs, and self-deceptive stories he tells himself—about himself.

You have the right (and the responsibility) to govern yourself (your choices, feelings, behavior, wants and needs). Know that your mate is going to viciously resist your efforts to reclaim your power.

Hence, you will have to discern when to disengage and no longer share your thoughts or feelings with your mate.

You can do this by saying one of the following statements:
- "No, I would rather not."
- "I don't see things that way."
- "I did not agree to that."

By disengaging, you begin to own, soothe, trust, and validate your own reality—over that of your narcissistic mate's.

You must outright reject the notion you can engage in interpersonal conflict repair or emotional discussions with your narcissistic mate—and continue to work on recognizing her various forms of manipulation.

As one of my clients so accurately said after I validated his abusive reality, "Once you see it, you cannot unsee it."

Start putting yourself first in your life—and act as if you matter—by consistently disengaging and recognizing the manipulation. When your mate attacks, step back or leave the house. But know that once you begin to disengage, your mate is likely to intensify her abuse. Your anxiety may increase—as you anticipate your mate's potential reactions. Your anxiety is largely the result of how you think your mate might punish you.

You may also feel guilt for planning to leave and not telling her. Whether you feel anxiety or guilt, know that these are your emotions to manage. It is critical that you challenge your feelings that you are being deceptive—and acknowledge the truth. It is your responsibility to put yourself first, by keeping your feelings to yourself. You are not responsible for the feelings of your narcissistic mate. Do not let your fear of retaliation stop you from making *the* only healthy choice before you.

This process involves admitting you cannot help or change another human being. With this acknowledgement, you can admit that the only person you can change is yourself.

You must remind yourself that your mate is not capable of listening, hearing, understanding, and accepting your emotional needs, nor is she capable of taking responsibility for her own caustic, angry, and manipulative words.

By disengaging—and no longer explaining, justifying, proving, or convincing—you are actually confronting your need to please head on—by catching yourself when you feel the need to "step in" and engage your narcissistic mate. This is disengagement—a critical piece to the process of detachment and letting go of the hope your mate is going to, someday, treat you better.

Every morning, it may be useful to consistently remind yourself that you are not who your mate says you are—and that she is not right about you.

It may be helpful to acknowledge the following reality of your abusive relationship:

- *My relationship is abusive—even though it may be hard to admit this to myself.*
- *It is never going to get better—in fact—it is getting a hell of a lot worse.*
- *I've got to quit trying to convince myself that things are going to change.*
- *Her abuse is only ramping up.*
- *I cannot keep kicking the can down the road.*
- *If I do, I am giving even more power away.*
- *She's got no desire to work on herself, or the relationship—and she never will.*
- *It is my responsibility to regulate my emotions and work on myself.*
- *Her anger is her responsibility. I am doing nothing wrong.*
- *Nothing I do will ever be good enough.*
- *She is literally devouring me—my energy and autonomy.*
- *She wants only to control me, punish me, and humiliate me to be an inadequate love partner.*
- *She's always got a problem with me.*
- *No amount of morphing and pleasing will ever make a damn bit of difference.*

- *In fact, it has made things a hell of a lot worse.*
- *We're clearly not in this together.*
- *I'm terrified of rejection, devastation, and believing I'm not good enough to get anyone else.*
- *I have the power to release these negative beliefs about myself.*
- *The idea of letting her go is so painful—but there's no other way.*
- *She clearly does not love me.*
- *I cannot stand the thought of her being with someone else.*
- *She is not my possession.*
- *I'll go crazy if I don't get out.*
- *I've got to make a legal plan to escape and serve her if necessary— before she even knows what I'm up to.*
- *The abuse isn't my fault—but I am responsible for tolerating the control and manipulation—and believing my illusion that things will one day get better.*
- *I'm not a victim.*
- *If I want a shot at a better life—to be happy and protect my kids—I've got to get out.*
- *I trust I'm making the right decision—and everything's going to work out for me and the children"*
- *The kids have been absorbing this negative energy in this house for years—and it is clearly harming them by remaining together.*
- *I trust that everything is going to work out now that I'm making the right, responsible decision.*

It is only when you put yourself first and get brutally honest with yourself—by deciding you want to create real change in your life, that you can cut through your rationalizations, excuses, and denial—and into the reality of your one-directional, parasitic relationship.

Often, once partners have made the reasonable decision to escape, they often feel guilty for now "living a charade"—and having to pretend— as they simultaneously keep their distance and hide from their mate.

They may feel that they have to be on high alert—and guard against her finding out—fearing what her reaction might be if she did. Sometimes, men even feel repulsed at this time—as they now cannot "unsee" who their mate really is. These feelings of guilt, fear, and repulsion are perfectly normal—and must be confronted and released if you are to begin to regulate your own emotions.

You must go through the motions (and emotions)—until you are out. You must accept that the road to happiness, emotional intelligence, trust, fulfillment, self-respect, self-worth—all involve emotional regulation of your feelings. And by putting yourself first, and releasing your need to please, you are doing just that.

Once you escape—and are living in your own home (with shared custody of your children)—your self-respect immediately increases—and at the same time, your feelings of guilt dissolve rapidly. By turning the mirror around—and now focusing on yourself—you are taking more power back and taking your first subtle steps towards escape.

While pleasers are often terrified as they prepare for escape, it is their beliefs about themselves—of who they are, what they are capable of, and what others are going to think—that create the majority of their inner conflict, fear, and feelings of inadequacy. Many actually tell themselves that no one else would want them—and this is all they deserve.

Fortunately, negative beliefs can be changed. How you think about yourself—and what you are capable of accomplishing—have so far been far too limiting. The negative stories you create in your mind reinforce your thoughts, feelings, and beliefs about what you are capable of accomplishing and overcoming in your life. It is these critical beliefs (and stories) you tell yourself about your worth and the horrible things she might do when you leave—that often determine what decision you make going forward.

Should you tell yourself you will be devastated should you leave—and ultimately lose your children—then you are less likely to choose escape. Like so many men, you will then choose the comfort of hell—and remain right where you are—choosing to "take it like a man," and hoping your mate will one day come around.

Your worry, mistrust, and negative stories you tell yourself about your future, may well inhibit you from making the courageous decision to detach, disengage, and legally strategize an exit plan. But now that you can look at your abusive relationship with new eyes, you can decide to make the only sane decision before you.

Begin looking for the good in your life—and what you have control over. The chain on the cover represents your need to please. You, alone, have the power to break this chain of pleasing—and legally plan your quiet escape. You *can* get out—and reclaim your autonomy, mental health, freedom—and create a better life (free of abuse) for you and your children. You *can* eventually attract a love partner who treats you better—because you will have learned to like, trust, and respect yourself.

How can you attract a loving relationship from a place of self-loathing and feelings of inadequacy? Yes, it is difficult to let go, and make sacrifices and changes in life, but it is necessary—if you are to eventually learn the discipline required to trust yourself. Imagine your goal of successfully separating (with a legal plan)—and what your new life will look like—as you take your next step out of your current comfort zone into a new comfort zone—to a better place in your life—where the grass is indeed greener.

Stepping from one comfort zone to a better comfort zone is precisely how emotional intelligence, trust, and internal strength is created and developed.

When you no longer forfeit opportunities because of fear and self-loathing, you begin to create more opportunities and possibilities as you push forward in life. Become aware of your critical nature towards yourself and acknowledge that both you and your children deserve better.

> Far too often, pleasers continue to ignore and reject themselves and, as a result, remain in ego, dependency, and low self-esteem. Refusing to exercise the courage needed to face their fears, they blindly ignore the truth—in favor of doubting themselves, feeling guilty, and living in fear. In so doing, their path of dependency (in the end) paradoxically, becomes the most difficult and painful path.

Living in fear and doubt, men unconsciously reinforce their situation, by doubting themselves:

- *What if the grass isn't greener on the other side?*
- *What if she seeks revenge?*
- *What if it is worse when I leave—and she withholds the kids?*
- *What if I'm devastated and cannot eat, sleep, or get myself to work?*
- *What if she's with another man?*

You can "what-if" yourself to death. The reality is, pleasers can be some of the most conflict-avoidant personalities I have worked with. They "what if" and worry themselves into doubt, depression, anxiety, and defeat. Pleasers sometimes internalize the abuse for years—until they feel too weak to do anything about it. They focus (with tunnel vision) on an illusion of a loving relationship, hoping to get back to a better place, while tolerating the hatred and manipulation of a toxic mate who only wants to hurt them.

So often, men are humiliated in abusive relationships—punished and beat-down for years—even decades. Most tolerate the hateful attacks for occasional scraps—a hug or even less—a reprieve from the abuse for a couple of days. Then, they sweep things under the carpet—and hope their mate will see what she is doing—and come to voluntarily stop her abuse.

Having worked with many, many pleasers (both men and women) over my seventeen years in private practice, I have come to believe that dependent, abusive relationships have a far greater purpose. I have frequently asked myself, "Why do narcissists and pleasers always attract?" I believe I have the answer. The pathology of the narcissist is so crippling and debilitating to the pleaser, he is ultimately forced to stand up for himself, or lose himself in anxiety, confusion, self-doubt, defeat, significant depression, or even suicide. Eventually, the pleaser is either forced to confront the pain of his deteriorating, abusive reality—or spiral further downwards.

The relationship either implodes—or he makes a far more courageous and proactive decision to begin standing up for himself—by admitting his abusive relationship is **hopeless**. Then, forced to confront his abusive reality, he becomes increasingly aware of his need to please and his deceptive belief that he has internalized all those years ago. He finally begins to accept that he is **not** responsible for the blame, anger, and manipulation of his mate—and never was. Until such time, the pleaser is merely playing out unresolved childhood trauma, abandonment issues, and feelings of inadequacy in his abusive romantic relationship. This is what he knows.

Just like he hoped his parents would eventually see him, treat him better, and love him more, the pleaser now holds to the illusion that maybe his abusive mate might do the same. Many cling to the illusion they can get their mate to treat them better (via pleasing), just as they did with their parents. Releasing this illusion involves confronting the unknown pain of separation, change, fall-out, grief, and perceived devestation. It involves facing and feeling the pain of letting go.

At last, however, the abuse becomes so painful and intolerable—or implosion occurs—whichever comes first. The pleaser's internal pain becomes so intense—the pain again literally forces him to confront his deep abandonment issues and self-loathing. His intense pain is quite literally his "Wake-Up Call."

At its core, this book is ultimately about personal growth. Getting out of a narcissistic relationship requires that you embark upon a journey of self-awareness and self-improvement. Eventually forced to flee from your humiliating, crippling relationship, you begin to look at yourself, and confront your disease to please. By focusing on yourself, putting yourself first, developing emotional intelligence, and adopting a positive mindset that fulfills you—you begin to trust, respect, and intrinsically value yourself.

Should you decide to turn the mirror around and begin focusing on yourself, you will begin to feel better about yourself—as you no longer seek to be filled by the few scraps of "love" your mate might throw your way.

The journey of self-reflection and seeing **who you really are** is the result of the powerful transformational inner work you are now undertaking—by reclaiming yourself (and your autonomy) through the development of self-awareness and a far broader understanding of narcissism and pleasing.

As we continue this powerful transformational process, you will come to see yourself as the powerful creator you truly are. As you begin to exercise the courage to trust yourself, you will know you are making the right decision. From this place of self-care, you can begin enriching yourself from the inside—and create a fulfilling life for you and your children. Once you acknowledge you cannot save anyone—except for yourself and your children—you will no longer feel exhausted, humiliated, lonely, and empty—but instead will ***push forward*** in the direction of happiness, confidence, respect of self, and freedom.

7

Reflections of the Inner World

In recent years, I have continued to see more abused men in my practice—some having tolerated their abusive relationship for more than three decades. As of late, I have been working with a man named Scott, whose wife, Naomi, put him on notice that she wanted a divorce. Naomi informed him she would seek a fair separation (which had initially provided some relief) because Scott had felt financially exploited for many years. Unfortunately, a few days later, Scott found a note in their vehicle—indicating Naomi was planning to go for significantly more money than she had previously told him—including half of his pension.

Scott informed me that his wife's abuse had escalated for years. When the couple first met, he ignored many red flags. Naomi was in significant debt and struggled with poor money management—in addition to battling depressive episodes—which tended to flare up more than he would have liked. Scott chose to overlook these issues—and figured he would solve all of these problems by taking care of his new girlfriend.

Hence, the couple rushed into their new romantic relationship. Scott was planning to *save* his new girlfriend.

Soon the couple decided they were ready to have children. Like many families, Scott would work and Naomi would stay home to raise the children. As years passed, Naomi's mental health deteriorated. According to Scott, she seemed to be looking for more out of life. Naomi took a stab at a couple of educational opportunities, but decided to drop out shortly after the courses began. She seemed to lack the motivation, discipline, and drive needed to follow through with assignments and complete goals.

When things were not working out for her, Naomi would use Scott as her punching bag. He recalled his wife leaving for a few days to visit her family—and how he initially felt a deep sense of relief to be free of her hurtful words. But the night before his wife left, he overheard a comment made to the children, "If your dad does not feed you, you tell me, okay?"

These words felt hurtful—and more than a little concerning—as Scott loved his children and made their welfare his top priority. But he knew he could not discuss his feelings with Naomi because, as Scott described, she was "hypersensitive to feedback." Hence, he coped as he always had—and shrugged her most recent comments off—without reflecting on why his wife might have made such a manipulative statement to their children.

While Naomi was gone, Scott noticed how peaceful he felt and how he enjoyed his time alone with his children. He was not aware he was being abused, nor could he recognize the manipulation.

When Naomi returned home, Scott noticed she seemed more irritated and depressed than usual. When he asked what was bothering her,

Scott found himself on the receiving end of deflection and criticism, noticing his wife no longer seemed to appreciate anything about him.

As Scott unpacked his thoughts and experiences, he disclosed he had married a project he had hoped to save. In hindsight, he realized that this had not been a good idea. Scott told me he had been *living on hope* for more than three decades. For the last several years, the abuse had ramped up to frequent accusations he was cheating on his wife—to which he had accommodated by staying home more—and no longer talking to other women. More recently, the accusations of infidelity had morphed into increasing financial exploitation and allegations Scott was neglecting his own children. The weight of the control, abuse, and increasing financial exploitation was crushing him. Accusations had turned into a manipulative campaign to buy her increasing expensive toys.

Naomi had always loved new, classy, items—like $100,000 vehicles. Scott would ultimately be expected to purchase these luxurious possessions for Naomi—and told he would be a better husband once she received these lavish gifts. Despite his better judgement, Scott would cave to his wife's coercive manipulation. Naomi would be happy for a few days—before returning to her abusive patterns of accusations and insults. Eventually, there would be another pressure campaign—and an expensive purchase required.

When Scott could no longer justify, or afford his wife's lavish demands, Naomi became increasingly abusive—with no regard for whether the children were witnesses to these hostile interactions.

Recently, Scott had been driving his wife to work, when Naomi lambasted him for being such an "abusive" man and "cheating" on her for so many years. Despite Scott's repeated requests to stop, Naomi snatched Scott's phone from the console—to search his most recent calls and texts. Having hit his limit from the verbal battering, Scott pulled over and attempted to grab back his phone. Naomi resisted—and there was a struggle that left Scott with scratch marks on his hands and forehead. Naomi then opened the passenger door and began screaming, "My husband is assaulting me! Help! My husband is assaulting me!"

Fortunately, Scott thought to exit the car and record his wife making these accusations.

After this most recent abusive episode, Scott retained a lawyer to move forward with divorce proceedings. He would soon be informed that a security camera had recorded the incident—clearly showing Scott had not assaulted his wife.

In the days following, Naomi threatened to charge Scott with assault. He felt that because he had recorded the incident—and informed her a security camera had caught them on tape—this deterred his wife from making good on her threats. After the incident, the couple decided to physically separate, but co-parent out of the same home. One parent would live elsewhere for one week and then alternate roles.

After listening to Scott's story, it seemed obvious to me that Naomi was entitled. She believed she deserved whatever she wanted, whenever she wanted it, without having to earn it. She felt that Scott's money was her money—as if he owed her whatever she wanted, whenever she wanted it. Despite the fact that Naomi did not have a job, the children were young teenagers, and she was not interested in working, Naomi felt comfortable exploiting her husband's finances—with no regard for his wants, feelings, or needs.

Naomi was entitled, yet did not see herself as entitled. She had a victim mentality—and believed the world owed her. Just like Naomi, your narcissistic mate also does not see herself as entitled. Instead, she believes (without evidence of any kind) that she is superior to most everyone else because she has gone through what she has—and knows more than others. Life has wronged her and therefore she deserves special treatment—without having to earn it—or make it happen on her own. It should be given to her because of the terrible hand that she has been dealt.

Feeling she has been denied a "good" life that others have been so privileged to receive, the narcissist believes her husband owes her for the misery she has had to endure—and for the "horrible" treatment he has put her through.

Because she feels "ripped off" from an easy life—that so many others have been blessed to have—the narcissist has developed a caustic and bitter attitude towards everyone—as if to say:

- "I've had it so much worse than you."
- "Who the hell are you—to tell me what to do?"
- "I know better than you."
- "I am smarter than you."
- "I am better looking than you."
- "I deserve to be treated like a queen."

Your narcissistic mate goes through life with a chip on her shoulder—as if to say: "Nobody is ever going to control me, or to tell me what to do again." Feeling as though she is being attacked, she projects the abuse of her parents onto others. Because of deep insecurities, she has no compassion for herself (or others)—and remains paranoid that others are out to get her—or are somehow trying to control her. She cannot see that people's responses are but a reflection of her treatment towards them.

Blind to herself—and deeply paranoid about what she believes others think of her, the narcissist obsesses over certain individuals that (according to her) do not deserve to be where they are in life. They have had it so easy—a loving family, easy education, and a successful career that they have not earned. She sees them as "incompetent" and unworthy of their success—especially because she has endured abuse and been through all kinds of hell and back. Life has given her a raw deal—and everything seems to be so hard for her. The narcissist cannot understand why she cannot catch a break.

Yet she complains incessantly about how screwed up people are and hates that others might enjoy success that she feels they do not deserve. The fact that she might have to listen to a boss who knows "less than her"—or thinks differently—is enough to send her into a tailspin of spite, and feelings of injustice. Feeling invisible, the narcissist goes through life, fighting to be seen, heard, and understood. Yet, she cannot trust her own perceptions—or keep her bitter feelings of injustice to herself. She needs to call people out—so they can see how "stupid" and "unfair" they are behaving. Hence, she fights, argues, and attempts to coerce others to agree with her—even though she is simply projecting stories she has made up in her own mind.

Desperately needing recognition, validation, and understanding—without caring what she says, how she says it, or how others might feel—the narcissist shames others for their careers, successes, and accomplishments—because she does not believe they deserve the success they enjoy.

In her anger and vitriol regarding how she has been overlooked, questions are falsely perceived to be accusations of incompetence. Disagreements to be attacks. Suggestions to be orders. Autonomy to be rejection or betrayal. The narcissist's insecurities, self-pity, and self-loathing create a myriad of projections and false perceptions about what others are intending, saying, and doing.

Things that have nothing to do with her are taken personally—or out of context. Living in paranoia—and hatred for authority—the narcissist cannot see what others are trying to communicate because comprehension requires emotional awareness, empathy, care, compassion, and feeling emotions.

Your mate is entitled—and sees herself to be above others. According to her, you **must** believe her phony persona of mental health and righteousness is actually her authentic self. Since there is only one "right" way of seeing, thinking, and behaving, you must agree with your mate's thoughts—and meet her every need need—so that she can believe her delusional perceptions of herself.

Unfortunately, your mate is hypersensitive about whether you truly believe her—and whether she believes you are being honest with her. Your mate only feels "secure" when you prop her up— and play along with her pretense—validating her false perceptions, caring for her, telling her how great she is, and going along with her financial exploitation of you.

For these reasons, your mate's abusive reactions, episodes, and attacks are highly unpredictable. She remains deeply suspicious as to whether you are actually being honest with her.

In Scott's case, he stopped interacting with women—hoping to quelch his wife's insecurities and false perceptions. He actually played into his wife's mistrust of him. Naomi knew, on some level, that she was forcing her husband's submission, yet hated him for "lying" to her. Clearly, Naomi's perceptions of herself (and others) did not match her abusive behavior and pathological cruelty towards Scott. In other words, her abusive words did not match her persona of who she perceived herself to be.

If an individual's words and actions are inconsistent, their words mean nothing.

Far too often, partners remain stuck in self-doubt—about whether their mate is her persona—or the nasty person they believe her to be. Because they give their mate the benefit of the doubt—and often cannot recognize the coercive manipulation, pleasers frequently question their own interpersonal reality.

Should you find yourself lost in self-doubt and confusion, you may notice yourself asking the following questions:

- "Is she really the kind, healthy woman she claims she is?" or "Is it me who just happens to unintentionally offend her?"
- "Is it possible she is nice? And I'm just somehow provoking her?"
- "Is it possible that she's right about me?"
- "She says I'm the one who's abusive. Am I?"
- "If she's so nice (as she claims to be), how can she be so insecure?"
- "Maybe I am this awful, horrible person that cannot seem to get it right in a romantic relationship?"
- "I cannot figure out which side of her is real?"
- "I feel like I'm going crazy. Am I?"

Back and forth you go—over and over again—unable to trust yourself—for how many years now?

Hopefully you can now see through your mate's phony persona—that it is **not** real. Hiding in ego—in a false pretense of mental health—your mate believes she is her persona. Head in the clouds—and high above others—she believes she has the right to get whatever she wants—at your expense. She believes she has the right to take it from you—because of how "horribly" you have treated her—and how "awful" her life has been.

Your mate's claims of moral virtue and persona of mental health are all a pretense (her ego if you will). She must convince herself and others of how superior she is, via coercive manipulation. For her to believe she is who she claims to be—you have to believe it too.

If your mate were truly healthy, kind, and loving—she would not require your approval, frequent reassurance, worship, and submission to remain "stable," nor would she react by lashing out, accusing you of immoral behavior, or exploit you financially—whenever you did not say or do what she desperately needed you to say or do. Your mate would demonstrate patience, humility, acceptance, trust, tolerance, empathy, and understanding—virtues she clearly does not possess. Because your mate is pathological, she must control your perceptions and feelings about who she believes herself to be—and what she believes she is entitled to have (to make her happy.)

Frozen in an invulnerable and defensive state (resulting from childhood trauma), your mate does not look within. She was forced to protect herself from the manipulative power plays of her parents against a barrage of lies she was told about who she was—and what she was responsible for. Your mate had to somehow prove to herself—that she was not who her parents "said" she was. The manipulation she received resulted in an overwhelming sense of shame—causing her to believe she was fundamentally worthless, flawed, and internally ugly.

To defend against these deep beliefs—just above or below the surface of consciousness—your mate hides from herself in ego and feelings of entitlement—entrenched in the conviction that she is right about her judgements of other people. While she so busily judges and criticizes others, your mate worries, stresses, and obsesses about "what ifs" and worse case scenarios. Because she needs to be recognized and adored, she finds people terrifying and threatening. Judgements and disapproval trigger trauma and feelings of being misunderstood. Just like when she was a little girl—mistakes would be met with shame-inducing verbal assaults and now, should your mate perceive she is being judged or lied to, she attacks. Unconsciously, she beats herself down as she has some awareness her behavior is indefensible. But rather than own her mistakes, she justifies her reactions are caused by others—because they did not provide the recognition or agreement she feels so entitled to.

This is the shame your mate lives in. Hence, she hides from herself in ego—a persona of perfection—to guard against deep shame which she conflates to be "proof" of her worthlessness. To avoid feeling the emotional pain of any (and all) emotional triggers that cause shame (or an uncomfortable emotion), your mate believes she must prove you wrong—and you on the other hand, believe you must agree you are wrong—so she can trust her perceptions are accurate—and deflect any, and all, personal responsibility.

Having no ability to trust herself because she cannot discern what she is responsible for, nor is she aware her emotions are her own responsibility to manage and regulate. Your mate needs you to always agree with her—even though she is now shaming and humiliating you—just as her parents once did to her.

Your mate now conflates confidence, self-worth, and success—with fancy cars, large houses, designer clothes, expensive vacations, and other material possessions. She believes that once she has all the material trappings of life, she will then be adored and respected by others. Just like Naomi, once she receives her external desires she believes will make her happy, she thinks that all of her worries and woes will vanish.

It is at this juncture, most pleasers I have ever worked with tend to get "stuck." Each insist they can, and will, somehow get through to their entitled mate—hoping she will eventually see the error of her ways. They hope some magical day will arrive when they finally succeed in making their entitled mate happy. And when this day finally arrives, she will see how hard he has tried—and how much he has given—to care for and to save his mate. When she finally recognizes his efforts, she will see the light—and begin to give all of her undying love back.

He will have succeeded in his promise to himself to **save** his wife—and demonstrated how he never quit on love.

Allow me to save you a little time, energy, and sanity. Listening, understanding, accepting responsibility, and ultimately changing is not psychologically possible for a narcissistic individual—unless, or until, she has the courage to end the co-dependent relationship and begin the painful process of breaching her defense mechanism of anger. Unfortunately, most narcissistic individuals do not ever accomplish this—even after separation.

> **Living in deep feelings of shame, self-loathing, and emotional pain, your mate has no love, compassion, or understanding for herself and others.**

It is always—and in all ways—been about her. Your mate's egoic lens is pointed outwards at all times—because she has yet to begin (or accept the responsibility) of undertaking the painful, difficult process of turning the mirror around—and looking at herself.

In the ass-backwards, upside-down world in which she (and you) exist, your mate sees you as the "monster" and herself as the "saint." These are simply projections of a deeply traumatized individual—in which things are always perceived to be someone else's fault. The fact that you keep "failing" to change enough only disgusts her—as she now projects the hatred of her parents onto you. In the same way she believes a $100,000 car will make her happy, she also believes you will eventually make her happy—if you could only change and bend just a little more.

Because your mate hates herself, she cannot tolerate the pain of self-reproach, nor can she tolerate confrontation of any kind—as she would have to admit wrongdoing—something she simply cannot or will not do. Hence, she will not take ownership for any offensive or abusive attack and, as a result, cannot develop the insight to see where she is wrong.

You must decide to accept your reality—that you cannot convince your mate of anything. She must defend her false perceptions of herself—and you—at all costs. Your mate will not self-reflect—no matter how significant the evidence against her. She is that stubborn. Your mate can justify and trivialize any and all immoral behavior.

As you begin to see how psychologically damaged your mate really is, you will no longer compromise yourself. Know that each time you do, you abandon and betray yourself—in the hope that your mate might one day see you.

The following are just some of the "rights" your entitled mate believes she holds over you:

> **Right:** I have the right to my hatred, anger, and mistrust towards you.
> **Right:** I have the right to make you responsible for my hate-filled, manipulative attacks.
> **Right:** I have the right to exploit you financially.
> **Right:** I have the right to speak my "truth," even though it might crush you.
> **Right:** I have the right to demean and dehumanize you — with impunity.
> **Right:** I have the right to control and change you.
> **Right:** I have the right to tell you what you can—and cannot—talk about.
> **Right:** I have the right to tell you your perceptions, feelings, and beliefs are wrong.
> **Right:** I have the right to punish you whenever you do not agree with me.
> **Right:** I have the right to isolate you to make myself feel more secure.

These are just some of the "rights" your mate believes she is entitled to—and the basis on which she justifies her abusive words and immoral behavior. Within her entitled mind, your mate holds this set of hypocritical rights, in which all malicious intent is attributed to you—because she does not feel responsible for the ownership and regulation of her emotions. This has unfortunately always been your *job description*—assigned to you by your mate. And like Scott, you took on the job, hoping you would one day succeed in saving your wounded mate.

No one can save anyone from themselves. No one can change anyone else.

Your mate has made it your job to regulate her hatred of self—and you. Once you recognize and accept your mate is pathological and has zero desire to change (or work on herself), you may then accept that *you* are the only person *you* can change. Admitting to yourself that you do not have the power to change, fix, save, or to help your narcissistic mate— is accepting the reality that you cannot change another human being.

It is my hope that you stop giving your narcissistic mate the benefit of the doubt—and acknowledge there is no way you will ever be seen, heard, or respected in your abusive relationship. This job of loving yourself falls upon you—and can only be achieved by putting yourself first and making the right, responsible decisions in life.

Do you actually believe your mate likes, respects, and trusts herself? Can you honestly say you like, respect, and trust yourself—even as you tolerate such horrific abuse?

It is ultimately your responsibility to scrape the scales from your eyes— and see what the hell is going on within the lie that you are living.

Are you ready to do this? I have been letting you know the reality of abusive relationships. You can choose to be a "victim"—or you can get out and be happy. This process begins with reminding yourself what you are—and what you are not—responsible for. Be sure to tell yourself:

- *She can think what she wants about me.*
- *I am not responsible for her perceptions and feelings about me.*
- *I cannot control her thoughts, perceptions, and feelings about me.*
- *I know she is wrong about me.*
- *I can see how much of a mess she is.*
- *It is safe for me to trust my own perceptions and feelings—over her hate-filled words about me.*
- *I am no longer giving credibility to her perceptions and words.*
- *Her words are not consistent with her behaviors—and therefore mean nothing.*
- *I no longer care what she thinks about me.*
- *I trust it is she who is abusive.*
- *I know it is not me causing my own abuse.*
- *I can only be abused if I tolerate it.*
- *There is no hope to fix or save this relationship.*
- *I cannot change anyone but myself.*
- *My only hope lies in saving and protecting myself—and my children—and getting out.*

Once you admit to yourself that you are in an abusive relationship—you begin to do the very inspiring and empowering work of changing your own thoughts and negative beliefs about yourself—and ultimately, your reality.

You then consciously make the decision to pivot and psychologically disengage: *I'm not having another talk about the problems in this relationship—or whatever I have done "wrong" now. I will talk about superficialities and keep my feelings to myself. She is unable to listen to anyone's feelings or experiences, accept responsibility, reason, communicate, or be vulnerable. She has zero compassion and empathy. It is always—and in all ways—about her.*

Be sure to remember:
- ✓ These "talks" always end in exhaustion, circular arguments, and abuse.
- ✓ Her instability cannot be diffused, fixed, or calmed for any length of time—no matter what you do or how much you accommodate her.
- ✓ You will never get through to her.
- ✓ Her defensive walls of ego, entitlement, and invulnerability are impenetrable.
- ✓ She will never see, get, or understand you.
- ✓ She has never known you, nor does she have any desire to—because she has always made everything about herself.
- ✓ Emotional connection, comprehension, and empathy are needed to develop a relationship. She does not possess any of these attributes.

Can you accept just how psychologically dangerous it is to expose yourself to a chronically manipulative individual?

Once you accept that your mate is not going to change, you now confront the **permanent** reality of your mate's narcissistic pathology. You must now choose to face your own insecurities and negative beliefs about yourself.

Have you ever considered that your external reality is merely a reflection of your internal reality? Are you aware of your own negative self-talk, critical thoughts, mental patterns, beliefs, and stories you tell yourself—about your worth and the value you add to a romantic relationship?

I encourage you to honestly ask yourself the following questions: Do you feel you deserve (in your heart) to be loved in a romantic relationship? As you are? Without having to be perfect?

While your narcissistic mate makes frequent claims of moral virtue (even though she has no empathy, awareness, emotional strength, trust, humility, patience, or love to offer), she expects you to be a perfect version of whoever she expects you to be. At the same time, you are expected to agree with how "immoral" of a man you are—and in order to keep the "peace," you generally do.

On the other hand, you expect perfection from yourself—to feel worthy of being loved. You must be perfect and never make a mistake—to get your mate's approval, love, acceptance, and validation. You do not feel you have the right to make mistakes in a romantic relationship. Mistakes are "proof" of your inherent unlovability and worthlessness.

Do you believe you must be perfect to be loved? Do you believe you deserve to be loved in a romantic relationship? Do you believe that you are worthy of your mate?

Because of your own unresolved childhood trauma, you hold many negative beliefs about who you are, what you deserve, and whether you are worthy of a romantic relationship. And guess what? Your narcissistic mate is mirroring these critical beliefs you hold about yourself—back to you—via her abusive words. Her abuse then reinforces the already critical beliefs you hold about your own lack of worth—and lack of rights you do not believe you deserve in your abusive relationship.

Consciously or unconsciously, you already abuse yourself in your romantic relationship. The beliefs you hold about yourself (on an emotional level) are congruent with the abuse you receive from your mate.

Your mate, too, has a multitude of self-loathing beliefs—that manifest in paranoia, intolerance, hatred, jealousy, judgement, criticism, accusations and threats—as she projects all negative beliefs onto you and hides from herself—in ego and the comfort of entitlement and victimhood. In this pathological state of self-pity, your mate justifies using and exploiting you—feeling you deserve to be treated this way for the imagined crimes you have committed against her.

Because of the horrible hand she was dealt, she believes she deserves to be treated with more respect, even though she does not respect herself. And because of your own sense of worthlessness (on an emotional level), you accept the abuse—because you do not respect yourself.

Unconsciously, your mate feels like she was disregarded (like some piece of trash), by first parents, and later by lovers. Internalizing her rejection and abandonment issues to be the result of deep inadequacies, she hates her parents—and previous lovers—for creating these wounds. Unconsciously, however, she blames herself to have caused these relationships to fail.

In like fashion (because of your childhood trauma and previous romantic relationships), you blame yourself to be some unlovable piece of trash—and the reason your previous relationships failed. Your narcissistic mate mirrors these negative beliefs and stories back to you—via her abusive words. In short, you abuse yourself with your own negative beliefs, stories, and self-talk—and these stories you believe about yourself are reflected back onto you.

The core issue is this: neither of you believe you are worthy of love in a romantic relationship.

Both the narcissist and pleaser are desperate for romantic love and each regularly engage in a battle to change the other's perceptions—for the purpose of gaining acceptance, love, approval, security, and understanding. Neither have healed old trauma—by releasing negative beliefs and old emotions each hold about their lack of value in a romantic relationship—and neither possess the awareness they must first like, accept, understand, approve, validate, and trust themselves—before they can feel worthy of a love partner.

Deep down, each feel undeserving of love, acceptance, understanding, and positive treatment—unless they can appear "perfect" (perfection being measured by the positive regard of the other). The partner must be happy with them—and when they are not—terror of abandonment is ignited. And because neither can soothe this terror on their own, each need the validation of the other.

Of course, leaving an abusive relationship involves confronting the terror of abandonment. But facing this fear (with no self-esteem) is not at all attractive because it involves feeling even more pain (or so they believe) than the pain they are currently in. While leaving involves confronting pain, it does not necessarily mean the pain will be greater, but it does mean the pain *will* be different—and unknown. To face this unknown pain requires courage—and a leap of faith.

After all the abuse they have received, many still remain physically attracted to their mates. Some would rather convince themselves of what could perhaps be—as they remain addicted to their mate's looks and body. This contrast between her external beauty and internal cruelty keeps pleasers addicted to the hope their mate will change.

You may well have put your narcissistic mate on a pedestal because of her looks and body—and the way she made you feel when you first met. Perhaps you are caught in some ego-identity of savior, family man, or maybe you feel it is "cheaper to keep her"—as you attempt to avoid the financial pain of separation. Whatever your reasons (or rationalizations), you may *still* feel strongly attached, in love, trauma-bonded, and addicted to the illusion of what was, or could be. Perhaps, like Scott, when you spend money on your mate, she treats you better for a few days—only to revert back to her abuse a short time later.

You were "good enough" one moment. Perhaps you might be "good enough" again in the future? In this way, you have become addicted to the pursuit of a few "crumbs" of love you might receive here and there.

Whatever the reason, you may now feel exhausted and defeated from having carried the entire, one-directional relationship— having done all the emotional labor to keep your mate happy.

Whatever egoic identity, addiction within, or feeling you still hold, your rationalizations that your relationship is better than it is, or will be better "when"—is nothing short of a fantasy. By choosing to stay, you are choosing to endure emotional chaos, broken promises, mood swings, entitlement, denial, control, manipulation, barbaric punishments, and financial exploitation on a daily basis—while gingerly walking on eggshells—and abandoning yourself.

Are you *ready* to begin the process of ending your relationship? To become *ready*, you need to stop stepping into the illusion of hope, rationalizations, and excuses—and accept that you are sleeping with the enemy—a dangerous, narcissistic, entitled woman—who is hell bent on exploiting you until she is ready to throw you out like a piece of garbage.

Until you wake up to your abusive reality, you are unconsciously rejecting yourself—and the psychological and emotional needs of your children.

In my professional experience, there is no bottom to the punishment and abuse many pleasers will tolerate—before they simply sink into defeat—and the bomb goes off. Forfeiting the personal responsibility of accepting reality, seeking help, recognizing manipulation, standing up for themselves, lawyering up, and planning their legal escape— pleasers choose to trivialize their destructive reality because they do not believe they deserve a better reality and a better love partner.

Possessing little, if any, self-respect, trust, and care for themselves (self-esteem)—pleasers actively avoid confronting their abandonment issues—often at all costs.

Frequently giving their mate the benefit of the doubt and tolerating crushing control, many pleasers refuse to protect themselves from the increasing anxiety, depression, defeat, confusion, control, manipulation, and punishment they experience—forever choosing to kick the can down the road:

- "I vowed to stay with my wife through sickness and health—and all the ups and downs."
- "I'm staying for the children."
- "Being a father and family man—is a big part of my identity."

Do these statements sound healthy—against a background of years of accusations and financial exploitation—with the same patterns and dynamics repeated over and over again? Yes, being a father is a huge part of a man's identity (as it should be), but taking that responsibility seriously means protecting your children from abuse, legally fighting for shared custody, and getting your children out of these toxic dynamics—at least half of the time.

Sometimes, pleasers will ignore my professional advice about how dangerous their living situation is—and how close to implosion they really are, deciding against retaining a lawyer and getting the hell out as soon as possible. Tolerating crushing control, many pleasers ignore their own (and their children's) deteriorating mental health—and justify their decision to stay—just to guard against what they perceive will be more pain should they get out.

Such denial, rationalizations, and excuses are used to protect against the deep terror of perceived devastation, losses, and a myriad of other fears. It seems the devil they know—and the hope they cling to—feels less painful than doing something productive about their own abuse.

In essence, pleasers continue to adapt to a new, sinking level of "normal"—hoping they can be successful at making it through another day—and that tomorrow will somehow—some way—bring about something better. All this—to avoid confronting the reality of their abandonment and dependency issues—in favor of keeping their heads in the sand and giving their vitriolic mate the benefit of the doubt.

> **This is the hell that partners adapt or conform to—having lost any degree of self-respect, self-esteem, or autonomy they might once have possessed.**

This book is meant to be a "wake-up call" for men who are *ready* to do something about the abuse they experience—to get out and be happy. You have rights as a man and a father. Reclaim them!

This book is written for men who are *ready* to do something productive with their lives. You no longer have to remain in a life-long "prison sentence"—in which your mate is the judge, jury, and executioner. It is time to summon the inspiration and courage to stand up for yourself, lawyer up, and prepare to get out—*now*—without your mate suspecting a thing.

You have the right to your perceptions, opinions, choices, and feelings—as well as the right to your children, career choices, and financial prosperity. You must exercise your courage to take these rights back—in order to live a life free of abuse. You can *reclaim* these rights—by acknowledging your own personal power as a man—and beginning to think differently, honestly, and courageously.

Remember—at the end of the day, your entitled mate is only a mirror—reflecting back to you your own critical relationship you have with yourself. You, on the other hand, are a mirror to her—reflecting the abusive relationship she has with herself. As she beats you down, she creates more internal shame and self-loathing—unable to exercise the self-restraint needed to stop her cycle of self-sabotaging abuse. And as you slowly pull away, she is forced to confront (on some level) what she is doing to you.

Are you ready?

8

Crushed

While Rob was playing in the living room with his three young children, his wife Tracy entered the room with a container of food from the fridge—and asked her husband, "How long has this been in the fridge?"

"I just made it a couple of days ago," Rob replied to his wife.
"So, two days ago?"
"Yes, two days ago," Rob clarified.

Tracy exited the living room and went back to the kitchen, while Rob continued playing with his three giggly little children.

A couple minutes later, Tracy returned to the living room and repeated the same question, "So, the food in the fridge is two days old?"

"Yes, I made it the day before—when you were at the office working." Rob found himself irritated by the question, but knew better than to say anything. He was well acquainted with his wife's need for reassurance and validation—as well as her intense need for control.

Knowing he could not show any signs of impatience or frustration—let alone express himself—Rob kept his thoughts and feelings to himself. He was used to dealing with what Tracy referred to as her OCD. Pushing his frustration down, Rob thought to himself:

- *She was here the day I made the food.*
- *I don't understand why she needs so much reassurance?*
- *I hate feeling handcuffed—where I cannot say anything.*

In order to deal with the control issues of his wife, Rob would often have these little conversations with himself. He knew what he had to do to avoid an abusive beat-down in front of the children. He would have to bite back his feelings—and keep his mouth shut. Rob resumed playing with the children and kept a smile on his face.

"So, you're sure you made the food two days ago?" Tracy asked—as if nothing were wrong with her obsessive line of questioning.

My God, she's irritating, Rob thought to himself. *I cannot believe she thinks nothing is wrong with badgering me like this. How can she not see how irritating she is and act as if it's all so normal?* He wondered why he was still surprised by Tracy's obsessive behavior—after dealing with his wife for all these years. But Rob knew he had better keep his composure and happily answer his wife. Hence, he bit down (yet again) and repressed his growing anger inside—pretending everything was good. "Yeah, I'm confident the food is good, Tracy. I just made it two days ago."

Rob was sure to take a deep breath—careful not to show any negative emotions—even as he felt his temperature rise. His only hope was Tracy would now be satisfied with his most recent confirmation that the food was good to eat. Having tolerated years of intense control,

Rob noticed his tolerance was waning—and sometimes he wondered how long he could continue to "take it like a man." Turning again to his children, Rob thought to himself:

- *I know she's controlling.*
- *You'd think I'd expect it by now—or at least be prepared for it.*
- *You'd think it wouldn't surprise me—or bug me anymore.*
- *I don't know why it still drives me nuts, but it does!*
- *Just hold it together and hope she's done asking about the bloody food.*

Rob had accepted he had no "right" to his emotions, but noticed he was becoming angry by the thought of his wife asking again. A few minutes lapsed while Rob continued to play with his children (who were too young to recognize what was happening with their parents). He then got up and went into the washroom to collect himself. Rob took a few deep breaths and attempted to calm himself down. He hoped perhaps Tracy would one day see her control issues. But after all these years, his hope was deteriorating. If anything, Tracy was more comfortable than ever—making him responsible to validate her mistrust of self.

Just as Rob exited the bathroom, Tracy came around the corner and asked him yet again, "So, you're sure you made the food two days ago?"

Having swallowed the ridiculous line of questioning several times, Rob had reached his limit—and made the "mistake" of expressing his frustration. "When you came home from work—the day I made the food—two days ago—you saw that I cooked it ***that*** day. You keep asking the same question over and over again—and I've answered you how many times now?"

No sooner had these words been spoken, that Rob knew he had made a big mistake. With a piercing glare, Tracy wasted no time putting her husband back in his place. "Don't talk to me like that," she snapped. "You're being disrespectful and rude." And off she went on her usual vitriolic rant about how "rude" her husband was, how he had no "patience," and how his "aggression" was totally unwarranted. Rob was now being blamed for Tracy's harassing, mistrustful, obsessive behavior.

The children were now crying and pleading with their parents to stop arguing—even though Rob had already shut-down—in the hope Tracy would stop. He recognized that he had lit the fuse—even though he had merely expressed his frustration. Now he was mad at himself for being so "stupid" as to have said anything.

Rob blamed himself for having broken rank and violated one of Tracy's many "rights"—one that he was not privileged to share. He had reacted—and dared to question Tracy's authority. He had not remained subservient to Tracy's obsessive behavior—and kept up the **pretense** that his wife's behavior was normal.

Now unglued, Tracy continued her vitriolic rant:
- "You're such an intolerant man." (judgment)
- "You have no right to be frustrated with me." (entitlement)
- "I've done nothing to irritate you." (denial)
- "I have a right to ask you a question if I want." (trivialization)
- "You should be more patient with me." (projection)
- "I've done nothing to offend you." (denial)
- "You're being abusive." (projection)

On and on she railed—for the next several minutes—repeating the above abusive statements over and over again—with no regard for the children's anxiety and pleas to their parents to stop "fighting."

As she had always done, Tracy expected Rob to put up with her control, re-assure her mistrust of self, tolerate her obsessive questions, demonstrate limitless patience—and now accept the beat-down he had coming. Rob was fully expected to regulate his wife's emotions and behavior.

While Rob had eventually reacted to his wife's crushing control, he could not fully comprehend **why** he had. He knew Tracy's expectation was for him to keep his mouth shut, but could not understand why he could not hold it together one last time. Expected to remain calm, patient, and happy at all times, it had become his job to tolerate the squashing effects of Tracy's control, while at the same time, validating the insanity of her narcissistic personality disorder. Clearly, this was not his responsibility, but he had accepted this role early in the relationship—to avoid abandonment and loss. Like Scott, he had hoped to save Tracy—and that one day the control would disappear.

> A pleaser always put the wants, needs, and emotions of his mate before his own wants, needs, and emotions.

Rob was effectively regulating Tracy's emotions and behavior to "keep the peace"—and avoid his own abuse—in front of the children. Each day, he attempted the impossible—without knowing it was not possible, sustainable, or responsible for him to live in this subservient position.

> Rob stubbornly clung to the hope that Tracy would eventually see what she was doing—and make the necessary corrections to her behavior.

Deep down, Rob knew he should be getting out—but always kicked the can down the road (doing what good pleasers do) and then later blaming himself for failing to tolerate his wife's crushing control. Hence, Rob downplayed the abuse while, at the same time, hoped Tracy would eventually wake up and see her control issues. When this happened, she would then want to correct her behavior—or so he told himself.

This is exactly what pleasers do in narcissistic relationships. They willingly take on the job of regulating the mental health issues of their mate, while repressing their own feelings—for the purpose of "keeping the peace" and avoiding the reality that the abuse is permanent.

In so doing, men trade their mental health, identity, and autonomy—and tolerate crushing control—hoping to avoid the next attack. They trade their deep need for acceptance, love, and understanding for the "security" of an abusive relationship. In Rob's case, he desperately wanted the love and understanding of his wife—hoping he could earn it by pretending that her behavior did not bother him—even as he was being crushed by her control. His hope rested in becoming "perfect"—by never reacting to Tracy's abnormal behavior. If he repressed his emotions, he could control his mate's behavior—or so he thought.

Should you fall into this mental trap (as most pleasers do), you will likely make the mistake of tolerating the squashing control of your girlfriend or wife, fearing any response will be met with abuse. There is no defense against the narcissist's control (inside the abusive relationship)—except to "take it like a man"—until you eventually hit your breaking point and react (often in front of the children).

Instantly, you will likely regret your reaction—and blame yourself for screwing up and causing your mate's abuse. Then, as you are torched by your narcissistic mate for "daring" to make such a "mistake," you blame yourself for your reaction—as if you could or should have been more "perfect."

For such a terrible sin, you will need to be punished in the presence of your children, even as you try to comfort and protect them from the collateral damage of the abuse. Like Rob, your house is on fire—and more emotional labor is required to put the flames out—by once again, compromising yourself, apologizing, and going back to repressing your emotions.

First the control, then the humiliating abuse, and now the shame you feel for "failing" to hold it together in front of your children:
- "Daddy shouldn't have reacted this way."
- "I'm so sorry kids."

- "I shouldn't have raised my voice."
- "It's okay. It's okay."
- "Everything's better now."
- "Daddy won't get upset again."

You may then even turn to your mate (who is still ranting) and start apologizing (compromising yourself) for "causing" this most recent abusive episode—even though she has not yet to cool her jets.

Finally, after a proper beating—to ensure you never commit this "horrible atrocity" of expressing yourself again—your mate finally relents. Now, exhausted, beat up, beat-down, wracked with shame for harming your children, and "failing" to be perfect—you now begin the difficult process of picking yourself back up off the floor.

Not yet ready to accept nothing is going to change in your abusive relationship, you go back to the drawing board—to review the incident (as well as your behavior)—and try to understand why you keep reacting in front of your children—and why you cannot just hold it together? Your pattern of second-guessing begins:

- *Why do a few annoying questions seem to piss me off?*
- *Was the situation really as bad as I made it?*
- *Was my reaction worth it?*
- *Maybe I just don't have enough patience?*
- *I know I'm damaging the children when I react.*
- *This insanity is killing me.*
- *But I don't know why I can't just keep my mouth shut?*

Underneath the self-doubt and shame lurks a terror in the pit of your stomach—the terror she might leave and take the children. This thought creates pure terror! The terror you have always tried to avoid—by blaming yourself—and telling yourself you can do better next time to avoid another attack. If you can just be "perfect," you will eventually be loved by your abusive mate.

The terror of what she is capable of doing rocks you to your core. You have probably been in this spot a thousand times—in this defeated, beat-down, terrifying reality—hoping things will blow over without an implosion. Then come the humiliating thoughts of why you keep taking it—along with the nagging feeling that you should be getting out.

Having just endured an abusive beat-down in front of your kids, calmed them down, compromised yourself, and now waiting to see if you are "out of the woods" for the evening—you blame yourself for "failing" to do better—and back to convincing yourself you can do better next time—by being perfect.

After enduring the terror of your abusive reality once more, you are back in denial, hoping you will do better next time—by controlling yourself, repressing yourself, and biting your emotions back. Then, finding an ounce of hope in your most recent rationalization, you pull yourself back up off the floor once again—and back to the familiar thought-pattern of denial—lulling yourself back into your "comfortable slumber" of avoidance that says:

- "I will do better next time."
- "If I can just be perfect, she will have no reason to abuse me. I just have to control myself better."

As a child, you used the same unconscious methods, by "doing more," "shutting down," "being better," "freezing"—and squashing your feelings down. More morphing. More abandoning and betrayal of self. Now, as an adult, you behave the same way with your wife—as you did them—and give another piece of yourself away and continue down the road of decay—inching towards implosion.

Another day, another episode—in which you can only speak so long as you go along with the crazy-making pretense of your mate—while rejecting yourself, and doing the emotional labor of regulating her narcissistic behavior.

The obvious $64,000 question is this: Why would you, or Rob (or any man for that matter), choose to take this kind of insane treatment day in and day out? Why would anyone choose to abandon themselves to this extent, and choose to live in this type of powerless reality?

In my years of practice, I have observed the unfortunate reality of codependency—in all its dysfunctional glory. Rooted in fear, self-doubt, low self-esteem, and massive self-deception, pleasers are, unfortunately, far from honest with themselves—in discerning whether they are decaying in an abusive relationship or whether they need to get out. Most buy into the blame-narrative of the narcissist—at the expense of their own perceptions and feelings.

It seems the narcissist is not the only dishonest individual in the relationship.

Not trusting themselves, pleasers make the dangerous mistake of regulating their mate's feelings and perceptions of "normalcy" and "mental health"—all while rationalizing their mate will eventually get it—and see what she is doing.

For many, their terror of further abuse—or getting out—is so overwhelmingly intense, they shirk back into a slumber—and lull themselves back into a false sense of reality—which is ultimately the lie they know (deep down) they are living.

Most partners enter my office and inform me they feel "stuck."

After listening to their stories (like the one above) and guiding them into their feelings, I usually respond with a small dose of reality:
- "While you feel stuck, no one is ever stuck."
- "Individuals choose to keep themselves stuck in fear, worry, stress, negative thinking—and their abusive relationship."
- "You always have a different choice you can make."

- "Your choices and opportunities before you—involve confronting your fears and choosing the unknown pain of change. This requires courage."

It would appear that some clients would prefer a simpler, or perhaps—*easier* response. The choices I begin discussing in therapy—involve independent thinking and making changes to yourself. I inform clients that responsible choices involve confronting reality for what it is—instead of hoping it will be the way they want it to be. But, many run from the notion that the restoration of mental health requires one to leave a toxic relationship.

Often pleasers get stuck in "fixing" by submission—having "normalized" their mate's behavior as being not as bad as it is—until they hit the moment of truth—where no matter what strategy they use—they can no longer bend reality to their will.

The abusive relationship has decayed to the point of insanity—in which each partner rationalizes, minimizes, defends, denies, and kicks the can down the road—while those on the outside, scratch their head and say to themselves, "Why the hell won't he just leave already?"

Should you find yourself in a similar predicament, it is not as though reality has **not** been staring you in the face. You have simply attempted to twist it your way—by telling yourself you can "make it work"—under the crushing weight of control. Yet, eventually, the moment of truth arrives—whether you want it to or not—and all the lies you tell yourself simply will not cut it anymore—no matter how terrified of change you are.

The solution to your own abuse does not lie in controlling your reactions to the point of extinction. Have you considered that pleasing, pushing your feelings down, and walking on eggshells might be your own control issues—to avoid the perceived pain of separation?

Your terror of change, perceived devastation, grief, fall-out, being alone, knowing your mate is free to be with other men, and whatever other fears you hold—are why you tolerate your abusive relationship. Your abandonment issues are essentially all your fears that must be faced to let go of your control.

You must get radically honest with yourself and face your fears— by exercising the tremendous courage it takes to let go.

Can you begin to accept—that you alone can confront your fears. Only you have the power to accept responsibility for all the changes you need to make—to resolve your abuse and heal your abandonment issues. Can you accept it is your job—and your job alone—to regulate your emotions?

By accepting the reality that your abusive relationship is ultimately destroying your mental health (and that of your children's)—you confront the false premise (lie) that you are doing the "right" thing by keeping your family together.

Since planning and preparation are necessary prior to escaping an abusive relationship, the time has come to actively practice psychological detachment—by accepting you cannot make your mate treat you better by walking on egg shells. Should you now be *ready* to accept this truth, you can quietly begin this process (and play your own game of sorts) in which you pretend all is well, while consciously detaching and disengaging whenever possible.

Once you get honest with yourself, lawyer up, and quietly make your plans to escape—the weight of control becomes bearable—in that you know it will only be temporary from here on in.

I have observed that many pleasers notice the severe control issues of their mate, yet, even then (like Rob) they hope they can stabilize their mate by ignoring their own feelings and pretending everything is good—until, of course, they react. Eventually, they hope their mate will see her immoral behavior and voluntarily stop the abuse once this happens.

Is this not hypocritical on the part of the pleaser—that he rests his hope on his narcissistic mate changing—so he does not have to experience the pain of letting go?

Hoping your narcissistic mate will eventually develop the insight she needs to regulate her emotions and behavior is a pipe dream. Yet, this is the fantasy world in which pleasers choose to reside—a self-deceptive reality that involves sticking it out long enough to see their mate change—or work on herself once she sees that she is abusive. When the pleaser chooses to cling to this "hope," he demonstrates he has no more desire to heal than his narcissistic mate.

Until you choose to accept it is *you* that will need to change, you will keep yourself "stuck." There is no one to blame. Your hands will be tied, while your perception of yourself becomes invariably anchored in your mate's deceptive reality—because you allow it. Over time, your feelings of guilt, shame, self-doubt, and negative self-talk intensify— even though you know (deep down) you are making the irresponsible decision to stay—while attempting to convince yourself you are doing the right thing.

Your mate's control mirrors your parents' control—and your own unconscious (or semi-conscious) beliefs about your capacity to be loved in a romantic relationship. Simply put, you are still living in an unhealed traumatic state of unlovability—having not yet learned to stand up for yourself and put yourself first.

Partners tolerate the abuse because, inwardly, they abuse themselves. Feeling as if something is fundamentally wrong with them, they take it—often believing they don't deserve any better. Keeping these negative beliefs to themselves (about how undeserving they believe themselves to be), partners compensate by trying to be—by morphing themselves into whoever their mate needs them to be.

Pleasers who refuse to get honest with themselves prefer to put all the blame onto the narcissist, while accepting no responsibility for the role they play in refusing to stand up for themselves. Luring themselves back into a false sense of security—they hope that just maybe the abusive episodes will somehow stop if they can just be a little better.

Conversely, pleasers continue to blame themselves for causing their mate's abuse—and try to fix the relationship by doing a better job controlling their own reactions—as opposed to exercising the courage to step out of their current comfort zone into a better one. Because of their own tendency to fret and worry, they think things will actually get worse should they leave. Trapped in their own negative mindset, pleasers decay into depression and defeat—telling no one about the abuse they endure—and trivialize their reality to avoid the pain of abandonment.

Is squashing your own emotions—under the weight of daily control—really "easier" than focusing your energy on something more worthwhile and productive? You!

Each time you are battered, you feel shame about staying—and subjecting your children to your reactions and the resulting abusive episodes. You doubt who you are and take on increasing amounts of shame about yourself and your capacity to be loved.

If Rob had fully accepted that Tracy was not going to change, he could have predicted that she would badger him with ridiculous, obsessive questions. Had he accepted he was powerless to change his wife, he could have accepted the reality that he could only save himself. Deep down, he felt like a coward for staying, but felt too weak to leave. This inner conflict made him feel like an abject failure as he wrestled with his guilt and mental anguish.

The majority of partners in abusive relationships erroneously assume that the pain and grief of leaving will be worse than the pain of staying.

This is life inside a narcissistic relationship—in the binary world of dominance and submission. In their tormented minds, many men make the wrong decision to ride it out. Even after seventeen years of private practice, I remain surprised at the volume of pleasers who come in looking for help—but do not want the help they need.

Many want some "professional secret" to save their relationship—as if an abusive relationship can be saved. Yet they often don't wish to look at the real problem, which is low self-esteem. The following are some of their beliefs:

- I don't deserve anyone better.
- I'm too weak to do anything about my abuse.
- Who would want me?
- I'm terrified to leave and grieve.
- I'm terrified to start over.
- Who will have my back if something bad happens?
- Staying in the hell I know is easier than the alternative of change—of facing my fears, uprooting insecurities, grieving, releasing negative beliefs, dealing with the fall out, and being alone.

In pleasing terms, this usually means: *I fear the pain will be more if I leave.* It is the ***pain*** they are trying to avoid.

The reality is—the majority of pleasers grew up in homes where power plays were the norm. They were not permitted to question their parents, have an opinion, request protection, or engage in attempts to repair conflict. Invisibility was required to psychologically survive. Approval, validation, and love were sparse. These precious resources had to be "earned." Having not had their emotional needs met, these individuals entered adulthood with deep insecurities and beliefs they had to be "perfect" to feel deserving of love.

Having experienced emotional abandonment, rejection and/or abuse as children, pleasers have old emotions, wounds, and deep beliefs about themselves (often unconscious). The two most pronounced beliefs that they hold are always triggered when conflict is experienced are:
  (1)   "Something is fundamentally 'wrong' with me."
  (2)   "I must have done something 'wrong.'"

As children, acceptance and emotional availability were rarely experienced—and individual autonomy was not permitted. Hence, compliance was the order of the day. These children could not learn how to validate their own emotions without the emotional support of their parents. Shamed whenever they did not meet the unrealistically high expectations of their parents, these children learned to work for love. They learn to earn it.

This is how their deep-rooted pattern of pleasing (giving, submitting, caring, saving, doing for, and trying harder) was developed. This is how these children emotionally survived—and how they protected themselves against rejection, control, manipulation, and abandonment. These same methods are still being used in their abusive relationship—to compensate for feelings of worthlessness they now carry as adults.

In the same manner they used to cope as children, pleasers trivialize the destructive effects of their abuse—and abandon themselves in the process. They rationalize they can eventually earn their mate's love, trust, respect, and validation—just as they had hoped to win their parents' love, trust, respect, and validation.

Hence, partners bend over backwards and submit themselves to regulate their mate's behavior and earn her approval. Rejection, abandonment, and abuse are simply too painful to experience—even more so, because the beat-downs are usually internalized. Believing (on an unconscious or emotional level) it is they who have "done something wrong," pleasers blame themselves for "causing the conflict" even though they cannot figure out what it was.

Because pleasers have not yet healed and uprooted their insecurities—by setting boundaries, releasing the need for parental approval, and confronted their fear of rejection—they have not yet developed the necessary self-esteem to recognize that it is not them causing their mate's anger. Fundamentally critical of themselves, pleasers frequently blame themselves for the negative emotions of others. This, by far, is the biggest error pleasers make.

In order to protect themselves from abandonment, and the fact that they will blame themselves for yet another "failed" relationship, pleasers often rationalize the relationship is better than it is—and will one day get better. And while they trivialize their abusive reality, their self-worth is eroded because of the shame-inducing abuse—and because they refuse to do what they know they should be doing.

> **Pleasers actively avoid the perceived pain of separation. The disease of pleasing is a maladaptive coping strategy—used to avoid self-blame for having "caused" another's negative emotions. Even though he may know (on a cognitive level) he has done nothing wrong—on an emotional level, he believes he is somehow at fault.**

The pleaser then rejects his own feelings—and makes an effort to please his mate—to make himself feel better. Pleasing elicits potential feelings of validation and love. Getting this external validation soothes the pleaser's internal anxiety and pain.

Only by facing your trauma and abandonment issues can you release your disease to please. This process can only be started when you are ready to get honest with yourself about the destructive dynamics of your relationship (for all involved), and challenge the blame you inflict on yourself.

Do you remember some of your childhood dynamics? You may have been blamed for making mistakes, or doing things "wrong" as a kid—followed by parental neglect, disapproval, judgment, shame-inducing rants, or aggression. As you were blamed for something—when it was your parents taking their anger out on you—you now blame yourself for your mate's aggression.

It must be my fault. I must have done something wrong. This has become your "go to" thought pattern whenever you are faced with disapproval or abuse. Now, all these years later, you find yourself dealing with the same poisonous manipulation—in the same way you dealt with it back then. You are vulnerable to the powerplays of your mate, because of the manipulative preconditioning you experienced as a child.

Believing yourself to be responsible for your mate's anger and false perceptions creates anxiety because of your tendency to blame yourself. You are simply coping the way you did as a child—having never learned to soothe your fears regarding others' anger and rejection. Blaming yourself, submitting to control, and compromising yourself are the same methods of coping you use now. Your mate's words are making you sick because you have never learned to deal with your fears of conflict, aggression, and abuse.

Because you were abandoned as a child, you now emotionally abandon yourself. This is precisely what Rob was doing. But as he began processing his feelings and experiences in therapy, Rob learned he was not responsible for Tracy's feelings, nor was he causing her frequent instability. He learned that biting back his feelings—and ignoring his own needs and feelings—was never going to be a healthy coping strategy.

Within a couple of sessions, Rob came to see how much shame and self-blame he carried when he reacted to Tracy's crushing control. He acknowledged his shame about his internal reality, asking me:

- "What kind of life is this?"
- "What kind of example am I setting for my kids?"
- "Why am I really staying in this sick relationship?"

When Rob began to get honest with himself—and the reality of an inevitable implosion—he became inspired and motivated to get out. With some assistance, he understood that adapting to control was not possible or remotely healthy.

Yet, this is precisely what partners do—sometimes spending decades reliving childhood trauma in their present-day abusive relationships.

Until you accept your relationship is abusive—and will eventually implode, you will remain stuck in these same thinking errors, grounded in self-blame and denial:

- What's wrong with me?
- It must have somehow been my fault.
- Maybe I do have a serious anger problem.
- I keep saying I'll do better next time, but I always end up reacting or blowing up.
- Why can't I just tolerate her control and keep my mouth shut?
- The kids don't see her control, but they see my reactions.
- They might think I'm starting the fights.
- Maybe I am to blame.
- Maybe it is me.
- I know I'm playing a part in my own abuse by staying.

- I know my kids are being damaged by these abusive blow-outs.

Allowing yourself to be controlled is psychologically debilitating—and invariably results in you internally blaming yourself for your own abuse.

In Rob's case, he blamed himself for his reactions to Tracy's control—believing he could simply exercise more self-control in the future—as if his goal should be to become some sort of Zen master. If he could just be perfect—and give Tracy nothing to blame him for, he rationalized he could prevent her attacks. Hence, Rob attempted the impossible (day in and day out)—as he added more expectations (weight) onto himself—on top of Tracy's constant control.

If he could just become the perfect husband—and never do anything wrong. If he could just walk on those proverbial egg shells just a little better, Rob believed he could fix his relationship. He had never stopped to think about how crippling, maladaptive, and unachievable this goal was. Just like Rob, many pleasers believe this will be their solution to their abusive reality. If they can just get their own angry reactions under control, the relationship will get better.

Is this not the pleaser's control? By fully repressing his own truth, by ignoring himself and pretending his mate's abusive behavior is "normal," he can become "perfect" and save his marriage—or so he thinks. Learning to validate your own perceptions and emotions is a critical psychological task towards learning to trust yourself. Fortunately, this skill is never too late to learn. To do this, you must accept that your perceptions and feelings matter—and they are critical sources of information and truth about what is actually happening in your manipulative reality. You must now turn the mirror around and pay close attention to your thoughts, perceptions, and feelings.

You must accept that you will never be understood, validated, and accepted by your narcissistic mate—ever! Your problem in your relationship is not one of communication, nor is it a matter of constantly screwing up—as so many pleasers tend to believe. It is a matter of learning to respect and trust yourself enough to see what is truly going on. To do this, you must interrupt your need to please—and see it is your mate who is pathological. By standing up for yourself —and confronting the legitimate pain of loss, you put an end to your abusive reality.

So long as you avoid your fears of letting go, change, and feelings of abandonment, you are avoiding the legitimate pain of growth. This is pathological avoidance—and it is precisely why you feel stuck—right where you are—and why your self-esteem has been eroded to the extent it has. The only way of finding peace and happiness—is to walk through your fears and release them—by changing your thoughts, trusting your feelings, and persevering until you get to the other side.

It is only through the pain of separation and the willingness to be alone—that you can reclaim yourself, your power, and learn to trust yourself.

To be true to yourself and heal your abandonment issues, you must accept full responsibility for the regulation of your own feelings.

In my world as a therapist, so many men and women attempt to avoid the legitimate pain of separation—and attempt to take the "easy" way out to avoid this perceived pain. Paradoxically, this avoidance requires more mental and emotional energy than the decision to leave. Until they are ready to face this unavoidable pain of separation, these individuals simply abandon themselves by making the extremely irresponsible decision to stay.

The bottom line is this: You cannot stop your mate's need for control by simply "taking it like a man" and repressing your emotions, nor can you get her abuse to stop by being better, doing more, or trying to convince her that she is wrong about your intentions, words, and behavior. Hoping to change your mate is all about your own control issues and unhealed trauma. Can you accept this?

Can you accept that you are powerless to change anyone but yourself?

It is only when you accept that you, alone, are responsible for your emotional and psychological well-being (by learning to like, respect, and trust yourself), that you are ready to begin this process of detachment—and accept that you are responsible for healing yourself.

In Chapter 1, I stated this book would be a "wake-up call" for men who are ready to do something about their abuse. This book is written for the brave souls who are ready to **push forward** and **pursue happiness** and mental health. Are you **ready** to use your abusive relationship as a catalyst for your personal growth—and the development of authentic power?

The process moving forward is all about learning to trust your own perceptions and feelings—while giving no credibility to the false perceptions and lies your mate spits at you. We will continue to change the way you think—so you no longer blame yourself for being "wrong" or "stupid" for reacting the way you do.

As you begin to see what you did not previously see, you release your deep need for external approval. As you consciously begin to step back, detach, disengage, and lawyer up, you begin to reclaim your personal power—by no longer giving it away through submission and emotional repression.

Do not make the mistake of thinking your mate will not implode at any moment—should you decide to stay. In fact, generally speaking, I only see abused men after implosion—and often after their wives have pressed bogus assault charges.

At the end of the day, remaining in an abusive relationship is ultimately a decision to abandon yourself and settle for a hell that is worse than the perceived pain of leaving. To continue to expose yourself (and your children) to crushing control and manipulation is to give yourself away (piece by piece) and model a toxic romantic relationship for them. The mental health consequences for yourself (and your children) are severe, including PTSD, feelings of defeat, depression, anxiety, nervous breakdowns, suicidal ideation, and suicide.

Time is literally of the essence. Are you ready to take your power back? Is it time to accept full responsibility for your choices and your emotions? Is it time to do the painful (albeit necessary) work of standing up for yourself?

9

Living on Hope

Pleasers are extremely willful individuals—in that they will often not let go of their abusive relationship—until, or unless, they are forced to—by implosion, followed by accusations and charges. Letting go (or breaking their chains of pleasing, dependency, and abandonment issues) is simply not in their interpersonal repertoire.

Of course, pleasers do not always see (or own) their willfulness—because the acknowledgement of this truth can be painful. Instead, they are more likely to say, "I don't like to give up." Or "I'm not a failure,"—as if getting out of an abusive relationship is a "failure"—and not a success.

For the pleaser, it is much easier to spin insecurities into "virtues"—as opposed to owning and uprooting them. Releasing their stubborn willfulness involves the willingness to *let go*—confront fears, and move through the pain of change. Such changes involve stepping out of ego (of what he wants—or does not want) and into heart (what is right, responsible, healthy, and required for growth, psychological development, and true happiness).

This process of becoming conscious involves **choosing wisely** and making decisions based on functionality and morality, not simply on want. To change and grow involves making decisions to legitimately suffer and to persevere through that suffering—including letting go of people who are toxic. The comfort of ego is not something the pleaser wants to release. He would much rather cling to his dependent, abusive relationship, so he can avoid the pain of letting go.

Of course, this begs the important question. Why would someone choose to remain in a hostile, dependent relationship—(willingly tolerating control and aggression from a mate who is hell bent on destroying him) rather than stand up for himself and get the hell out?

The reason so many individuals feel terrified to make such critical and necessary changes to their lives comes down to fear, willfulness (ego), low self-esteem, and the avoidance of perceived, unknown pain. In the end, reality never budges—no matter how much the pleaser insists (hopes) it will. In his extreme willfulness, stubbornness, and resistance, the pleaser offloads personal responsibility onto his narcissistic mate—even though she has demonstrated zero desire to change.

The reality is—the process of changing our personality, or some aspect of our life, is often frightening and painful. For many, these required changes are unattractive and terrifying. In sessions, I am often informed:
- "That sounds too hard."
- "I don't feel strong enough to leave."
- "What if things get worse, not better?"

Some clients will literally begin shutting down at the very thought of making the critical, life-changing decision to escape—because of real or perceived losses, legitimate suffering, and the courage and trust required. Instead, they shirk back into their comfort zone, rationalizing they can fix their abusive relationship. It is right here (at this juncture) that many individuals simply quit on themselves.

Living in the comfort of a habitual hell, pleasers can often find no motivation to undergo the legitimate pain of change that results from making the right, responsible decision (not the egoic decision of what they want—or don't want to do). They are unwilling to commit to the sustained effort to plan, detach, disengage, regulate their emotions, follow through with escape, stay away, and persevere through their grief.

> This change process requires that the pleaser release his need to change the perceptions of his girlfriend or wife—and admit to himself, that he cannot change another, nor can he make the relationship work by doing all of the emotional labor himself.

The responsibility of change and growth, then, becomes the core issue of the abusive relationship. This individual change process comes down to owning, tolerating, and processing fear—and stepping into the unknown emotional pain of letting go. These are the first steps out of ego.

For many, the need for change is lost in the fear of change itself. This fear is so intense, they resist the required changes—through the use of rationalizations, excuses, denial, and avoidance (all forms of self-deception) to avoid the legitimate suffering of letting go and personal growth. In other words, fear stops them dead in their tracks.

This chapter is all about making such required changes. Assuming you have already lawyered up (or are about to), you are ready to begin this courageous process. The process is not simply about making a critical decision, it involves far more than that. The real work of change involves confronting and releasing your pattern of pleasing. In other words, each time you become conscious that you are about to engage in this pattern, you must resist the urge, pivot, and exercise self-restraint.

In order to resist pleasing, you must first admit to yourself that proving, explaining, justifying, and morphing yourself into whoever your mate wants you to be, has never worked, nor is it helpful for anyone involved. The acknowledgment, itself, requires **your willingness** to be true to yourself—and to admit there is no way in hell your abusive relationship is ever going to get better. You must acknowledge that the only way to improve your abusive reality is by working on yourself and battling your resistance. This process involves frustrating your need to please— which is to say—that you become aware of the compulsion, feel the compulsion, and resist acting on the compulsion. When consistently practiced, your need for approval begins to die—along with your fears of abandonment and worthlessness—as you build external strength and remain true to yourself. This consistent practice breaks the chains of pleasing—as you gain power by frustrating the need.

> **This process of frustrating your need to please becomes empowering—
> as you begin to respect and trust yourself in the process. This process
> of self-development feels so much better than submission.**

This process involves the implementation of invisible boundaries—in which you no longer share what you are thinking or feeling with your mate—or diverting from subjects you do not wish to discuss.

I am often informed by clients: "I can't do this. She will get angry."

So let me be clear: The goal of this technique isn't about avoiding your mate's anger, although disengagement might certainly help. Instead, this process involves detachment and learning to feel and process your emotions. This process is about stepping back—and no longer engaging in discussions of a personal or emotional nature. Depending on how close to implosion you are, you had better be ready to leave at any moment. Once you have your legal and practical ducks in a row, you will want to make your move immediately.

Disengagement and the process of frustrating your need to please is designed to build self-esteem—by resisting the need to "make things work" or "repair conflict" with your mate. You will have to determine at what point you are ready to begin this process—and learn to own, tolerate, and process your insecurities and anxiety when your mate becomes aggressive. You will need to resist pleasing behaviors by disengaging, walking out of the house—and battling painful emotions of guilt and fear. As a pleaser, this is a very difficult thing to do—because it is the first time you are owning and processing your painful emotions—without engaging in the insecure behavior to please.

> The most important piece to remember as you develop
> these new skills—is to be subtle. Your narcissistic mate
> will sniff out any changes you make to yourself.

The process of disengagement and invisible boundaries must be consistently practiced—no matter how hard it feels. This involves willing yourself (in counter-intuitive ways) to resist your natural impulse to please—by not "copping out" or reverting back to pleasing when your mate wants something. It may mean responding with "No, I'm not able to do that," without an explanation. But, you will have to assess how close to implosion you are. If your mate's level of control is through the roof, do not use the word "No" unless absolutely necessary.

Disengaging might mean leaving the house with an excuse of running an errand. Take the space you need and practice staying away—without letting on you are doing anything out of the ordinary. You must remain intentional about resisting your compulsion to please and engage in interpersonal discussions involving feelings—"hoping" you can work things out.

Remain on guard—and anticipate an attack at any time. When it comes, resist any compulsion to react and engage. This may feel like "taking one off the chin," but it increases stability in the home. Remember, you may not have a lot of time before escape is absolutely necessary. You will have to judge how close you are to a possible implosion—based on a number of factors, including increasing instability, threats, and mounting control.

The idea is to beat your narcissistic mate to the punch. By persevering through this process, you begin the process of personal growth—by battling your compulsion to engage in interpersonal conversations that require reason and emotional awareness. You are now in the process of changing yourself—as opposed to hoping your mate will change and stop her abuse.

You are now choosing when to engage—and when not to engage—as you now anticipate the outcome of each decision. No longer are you attempting to "make" your mate love you, or be the person she needs you to be. You are beginning to let go, step back, disengage—and release your need to please—all in very subtle ways.

As you work through this process, you may feel pieces of self-respect and internal strength building within—as you no longer give your precious energy and personal power away through insecure methods of communication. You are now honoring your feelings by remaining true to yourself—and no longer submitting to your mate's control. You now practice tolerating, processing, and soothing your emotions—as you acknowledge you are definitely leaving.

As you confront and feel your emotions associated with separation, you can work through the emotional consequences of your decision. In so doing, you begin grieving and implementing invisible boundaries—no longer participating in interpersonal or abusive discussions about how you are "failing" or "not doing enough." Communication beyond the superficial will end in your abuse.

Be cautious about using the word *No*—unless it is imperative.
It may not be appropriate if the risk of implosion is high.

Reacting when you are attacked will be tempting; however, each time you do, you step down to her level—and re-engage in an abusive battle that could last for hours. Keep the moral high ground—as you begin to work through your emotional experience of detachment and grief.

The process of detachment and disengagement may elicit emotions associated with grieving, such as, sadness and loss—but also feelings of guilt—that you are harming your mate, being deceptive, or mean for "letting her down." Know that these feelings are the result of low self-esteem—and the belief that you are responsible for other people's feelings.

At the core of pleasing lies a negative belief system about yourself—a belief that drives you to assume responsibility for the emotions and behavior of your narcissistic mate. Therefore, each time you are manipulated, feelings of guilt and shame flood through your body—and trigger an automatic belief that says: *I must have done something wrong or something's "wrong" with me.*

These same feelings of guilt ignite your need for approval—and the compulsion to explain, prove, and convince your mate you have not intended to offend her. These feelings of guilt must be challenged—by not acting on them and re-engaging with your mate. You are now strengthening your internal power—by using your will to let go of old emotions (like guilt) that no longer serve you.

In order to battle your compulsion to please, you must process painful feelings of guilt, abandonment, terror, shame, and grief. This is the emotional work of letting go—and the process of personal growth.

If your mate is making threats of leaving with the children, you should take these threats seriously—as these are solid indicators of what she is scheming to do. Should these threats be followed with accusations of being "selfish," "horrible," "mean," and "incompetent" as a partner or father, know these same accusations are likely to end up in an affidavit. But you can legally beat her to the punch by informing your lawyer of these accusations.

Beware: Now that you are choosing to stand up for yourself—and inch backwards from your mate's need for control—she will invariably begin to feel a loss of control over you. This means she will feel powerless—and become jealous and resentful of your increasing strength and decisions to disengage. **Be cautious.**

At this stage in the game, your mate could very well implode (as many narcissistic women do). This is precisely why your legal plan should be concurrent with your disengagement process and frustrating your need to please. It takes tremendous courage to stand up for yourself in the face of threats and accusations—and a fierce commitment to yourself—to do whatever it takes to free yourself, in order to create a better future. You have become "comfortable" in the pain you know—but as you actively engage in frustrating your need to please, you let go of caring what your mate thinks of you.

The abuse may begin to ramp up, triggering your compulsion to please. As deep insecurities and threats of loss (of the children) increase, so might your compulsion to pacify your narcissistic mate. Be aware you may be tempted to submit, but that will only take you backwards.

By challenging your compulsion to both please and submit—you begin to release (one step at a time) your need for approval. By pivoting and disengaging, you are interrupting the trauma bond and cycle of abuse—while at the same time developing emotional strength through resistance. This process is not going to stop the abuse, but you will not be reacting and engaging in it.

Should you receive an abusive text, simply don't respond. Should it be a phone call, you say "I'd rather not talk about this" and hang up the phone. Should you be insulted in your home, pivot and walk away (and leave the house if necessary).

Only once you accept your mate's psychological and emotional limitations, will you accept that you, alone, are responsible for your escape and for standing up for yourself. Detachment, disengagement, and the simple word, **no** (without justification), mark the beginning of personal growth—and soon, the end of your abusive relationship. This process builds discipline, emotional strength, self-restraint, and self-esteem.

> Having accepted there is simply no way to be—or way to talk to a narcissist (to gain acceptance), you are ready for change. You now anticipate the abuse—and immediately disengage when your mate wants something you are not prepared to give.

Using this process, you are developing a different mind-set and building self-esteem—by changing your intentions, expectations, reactions, responses, and behavior—with the ultimate goal of detachment, disengagement, and escape. As you practice these psychological shifts, you begin owning, tolerating, processing, and soothing your emotions on your own. By regulating your emotions (and not your mate's), you will be out the door before she knows what hit her. Stay a couple of steps ahead of her. If at all possible, make sure she does not get a sense you are planning to leave. If you get out prior to implosion, you significantly reduce the collateral damage to yourself (and your children).

Again, if you have not done so already, it is high time to lawyer up, learn your rights, and develop a legal exit strategy—including serving your mate once you are out the door. The more you are prepared mentally, emotionally, and legally, the better position you hold to gain shared custody of the children.

You are now putting yourself first—perhaps for the first time in your life. No longer are you lying to yourself about the relationship being better than it is, or taking the path of least resistance—at your expense. You have begun your process of changing yourself and of personal growth.

The process of personal growth involves legitimate suffering—and the responsibility of regulating your own insecurities, emotions and behavior.

This process involves forcing yourself to make the very decision your ego does not want you to make. But your heart knows it is the only functional and responsible decision to make—to step into the unknown pain required to reclaim your personal power.

Unfortunately, many individuals are highly resistant to such a significant change process—primarily because of the unknown pain they must incur. Instead, they lament how their problems are not their fault— and how hard life is—or even, how they shouldn't have to be the one to leave their home—as if ending an abusive relationship shouldn't be their responsibility.

On a regular basis, I am informed by clients that it is "easier to stay," than make the responsible decision to confront their fears, leave, and choose the legitimate suffering of grief. Yet, this is the only way forward—towards healing abandonment issues, building self-esteem, and escaping abuse—with the goal of becoming happy and free.

I sometimes ask clients:

- "How much mental and emotional energy does it take to remain stuck in an abusive relationship—and abandon yourself in the process?"
- "Do you feel you are losing yourself—and trading your mental health for the "security" of your relationship?"

I then reframe the true purpose of an abusive relationship—as it relates to the notion of personal growth. I share with clients my belief: I believe the narcissist is truly a catalyst for personal growth—as she forces the pleaser to confront his abandonment issues—by standing up for himself, letting go, and releasing his need to please.

The toxic relationship ultimately forces men to confront the following questions:

- Do you feel you deserve to be treated this poorly?
- Do you believe you have the strength inside to get out?
- Do you feel you trust and respect yourself?
- Do you know who you are?
- Do you believe in your potential?
- Do you trust yourself?
- Have you lost yourself?
- Have you abandoned yourself?
- Do you believe that you matter?

By confronting the answers to these questions, you can begin to look at yourself—and explore how you feel about yourself. If you are going to willingly choose to confront your abandonment issues—and develop self-esteem, you need to honestly answer these questions. Many men would rather avoid such introspection and ultimately be forced out of their abusive relationship at the end of the day—after implosion. At this point, they are forced to confront these issues.

You have hopefully arrived at the brave moment of truth—in which you lawyer up, practice disengagement, regulate your emotions, and beat her to the punch. Of course, getting to this point requires significant courage for a man who has never dealt with his own childhood trauma.

When you acknowledge your abusive relationship has nothing to do with love—no matter how much you may feel you love her, you are ready to let go and heal your attachment/abandonment issues, past trauma, low self-worth, fear of change, facing the unknown, and the terror of perceived, or real losses.

Facing these fears and losses (perceived or otherwise) and processing your own unknown fears—requires that you go to battle within yourself (in a good way)—as opposed to rationalizing your ego identity, such as:
- "We've built a life together."
- "I see myself as a family man."
- "I made a commitment—and I take that seriously."

Once you shed the thin veneer of ego, you begin the process of personal growth—and begin to face many insecurities—like the fear she will be free to be with other men—or confront your intuitive knowing that she already has.

I recently worked with a client who refused to accept his abusive reality for over two decades—even though he was well aware of his own abuse, and well aware things were getting worse. He maintained he was a "committed" family man—and planned to honor that commitment. Ten years earlier, his wife cheated on him—but denied it happened— even though he found lingerie by the bed that she had not worn in years. Deep down, he knew she had cheated, even though she denied it—without bothering to provide an explanation as to why her lingerie was on the floor. My client accepted his wife's baseless denials, even though he suspected otherwise.

For ten years, his wife told him to leave, accused him of being emotionally abusive—and suicidal. No matter what tangent she went on, my client would accept his job of regulating his wife's abusive behavior—even though these unstable situations would sometimes end in physical assault.

My client did not capitalize on the opportunity to charge his wife—and go for custody of his children. Even after frequent physical assaults, he hoped he would one day save her—by proving how much he loved her—and believing in her—that one day she would meet her potential as a loving mate.

Another abused man, eventually forced out of his abusive relationship against his will—as he attempted to avoid making the painful decision himself.

Deep insecurities, low self-esteem, and fears of significant loss keep abused men clinging to some illusion they can get back to where they once believed they were. Ironically, in their extreme avoidance, most abused men end up confronting their fears and losses after implosion, then find themselves on the defensive end of accusations and false charges in a legal affidavit, having to find a new residence, and fighting for shared custody of their children.

The whole separation process becomes more complicated and terrifying than it would have been had they faced their abusive reality sooner. It begs the question, how much of it could have been avoided if these men had confronted their abandonment issues and made the necessary changes when the writing was obviously on the wall?

Many abused men adapt to the insanity of daily abuse—as they hope to one day save their wife—by accepting and regulating her abusive behavior. This is nothing short of giving their wife a green light to abuse them.

The bottom line is this: You must battle your compulsion to please—and your own impulse to stay and submit to the ongoing abuse. You must get real with yourself and step out of your egoic wants—that insist you can "make your wife happy." Instead, you must take the first steps into heart—and decide what is right, healthy, and necessary for the mental health and sanity of all family members involved.

This dedication to reality—marks the beginning of a true desire (and deep need) to make both the obvious, and necessary, changes to yourself—and to your life.

Perhaps, for these reasons, the process of personal growth is so unattractive for many. It seems to be a last resort—one in which many find themselves (in insurmountable pain)—forced to make the responsible and difficult decisions after implosion. At this point, the choices are invariably the same. Nothing was avoided—and reality did not bend.

This is where so many pleasers go down the dark worm hole of decay and intensifying abuse—choosing to do what they want, what they know, and what seems easier—verses what is right—what is responsible, and what is healthy for all involved. Unfortunately, most pleasers do not ask themselves these difficult questions. If they do, they often shirk back from the fear of stepping into the unknown.

I have heard many pleasers ask the question, "How do I know the grass is greener on the other side?" They seem to require absolute certainty, before each would dare make the courageous and trusting decision to leave the comfort of their predictable hell.

As many doubt themselves and reinforce their irresponsible decision to stay, I often remind these men that they can learn to trust themselves and learn to develop a positive mindset—if they would just listen to their hearts—and step out of their egoic wants—into what they know to be true. This is how true freedom, trust, personal power, mental health, self-respect, and happiness is developed.

> **This juncture marks the beginning of personal growth. It is a difficult process to initiate—because it often is not started unless an individual is in intense emotional suffering. Pain is the initial motivator for growth.**

This process of self-reflection and making changes to yourself (and your life) is more powerful, fulfilling, and rewarding than you can possibly imagine. Ironically, at the same time, the change process requires that you willingly move out of ego and into your heart—from making choices based simply on what you want—to what is right, responsible, and healthy.

> **When these choices of the heart are made, you begin to embark on a much happier and healthier path in life— and just like that—you are no longer "stuck."**

As you read these words, you may well experience a variety of emotions. Perhaps guilt about this process of leaving and not sharing your plans—as if you will be "hurting" your mate or "letting her down." Conversely, you might begin to feel real hope and optimism—that a life free from control and manipulation awaits you. The truth is, you will be honoring yourself—by protecting yourself and standing up for yourself and your children—perhaps for the first time in your life. Experiencing new emotions and challenging old thought patterns are all part of the process of personal growth.

It is useful to remember why you feel emotions of guilt. Guilt is a form of manipulation—and it may well have been used to keep you in your place. As you developed patterns of pleasing to gain parental approval, you learned to take responsibility for the feelings of others.

Know that your mate's abuse is *not about you*, nor does it mean *something is wrong with you*—and it certainly does not *define you*.

In the big picture of life, we attract love partners to help us learn and grow. Whatever happens in our lives, happens for a reason. There is a lesson that needs to be learned. If you feel "stuck" in the hell of an abusive relationship, you yourself, have not yet begun to work on yourself, reverse the lens, and step out of ego—into a far more powerful process of living.

Since your narcissistic mate is certainly not about to change, it looks like it is up to you. The responsibility of making changes falls upon you—as it should. This is a blessing in disguise. You will either go down with the ship—until implosion—or decide to detach, disengage, self-soothe, and release your need to please. The choice is yours—until it is not.

You attracted your narcissistic mate for a reason—because you both have unhealed trauma that you have been replaying in your abusive relationship. However, in the end, you can use this relationship as a platform to heal, learn, and grow—to recognize that both pleasing and narcissism destroy love—and life—because both are dishonest methods of communication. Both are attempts to change and control the other.

Without a doubt, you have lost yourself in your narcissistic relationship, yet it is not too late to reclaim your power. Fortunately, you have choices before you. You can now choose to put yourself into the driver's seat of your life—and release your need for external validation.

To continue to require approval and love from a dependent, insecure, vitriolic woman—is to live with a ton of fear and anxiety about having to be perfect—all to avoid any possibility of rejection. Ultimately, this book teaches the skills and the strategies to build self-esteem—and to like, respect, and trust yourself. The quality of your life depends on ***this*** decision to process and regulate your own emotions—and not those of your narcissistic mate.

As you begin to make these changes, and persevere through the difficult times ahead, you will notice that you are growing in feelings of relief, respect, strength, and trust. Submission, personal compromise, and the toleration of abuse are no longer options. It is no longer a part of who you are. Your abusive relationship no longer serves you, nor does it warrant your time, energy, and focus. You cannot "unsee" what you now "see."

As you are about to learn, the most important battle ahead—is within yourself. And this is precisely where we are headed.

10

The Enemy Within

Would it surprise you to know that—up until this point in your life—your real enemy has been fear and low self-esteem? That each time your mate spits venomous manipulation, you have internalized many of her lies against you? That you have come to believe them on an emotional level—even though your head knows differently?

Having internalized so many of your mate's lies, you might not even notice the many lies you tell yourself. Do any of the following sound familiar?

- "Something's seriously wrong with me."
- "I'm too weak to leave."
- "I'm disgusted with myself."
- "I can't believe I lost it in front of my kids again."
- "What kind of a man tolerates this crap—and keeps making the same stupid mistakes over and over again?"
- "I'm so f…..g worthless."
- "I'm not good enough."

- "If I leave, I'm not going to find anyone else."
- "Who's going to want me?"
- "I don't deserve to be treated better."
- "She's all I deserve."

First, your narcissistic mate attacks your character with lies. Then you lie to yourself—telling yourself that you are worthless and too weak to leave. As a pleaser, whenever you experience conflict, rejection, and coercive manipulation, you automatically believe that you were in the wrong—and that you somehow warranted the critical words of your mate.

Are you aware of your own negative self-talk—and the lies you tell yourself? Are you aware that you have been taking responsibility for other people's negative feelings about you for most of your life?

Are you not extremely critical of yourself? Your own worst enemy? That you automatically blame yourself when your mate becomes angry? As if you "made" her mad or "did" something wrong?

There is zero power in worrying about what others think about you.

Do you believe you can build self-confidence and self-esteem? Are you willing to release the self-deception that you are worthless, inadequate, or unlovable?

Your self-concept determines the quality of your life—and the quality of your relationships. It only matters what you think of you.

What if you no longer felt desperate to get love from your narcissistic mate? What if you exercised your personal power (the power of consciousness)—to begin releasing old, outdated beliefs—and replacing them with the *truth* about who you are? What if you reframed abuse and no longer believed it had anything to do with you?

All pleasers hold critical beliefs about who they are, what they deserve, and what they are worth. Quite simply, they don't believe they deserve to be treated well in romantic relationships and even question whether they deserve to be supported and loved. On an emotional level, pleasers believe their abusive mate is the best they can do. Hence, they focus all their energy on obtaining scraps of love—while ignoring and repressing negative beliefs about themselves. Yet, these critical beliefs become activated when guilt trips, insults, and other forms of manipulation are experienced.

When their mate attacks, pleasers often criticize themselves, thinking:
- I screwed up again.
- Why couldn't I just have kept my mouth shut?
- What's wrong with me?
- I don't deserve to be in a relationship.
- I'm too f***** up.
- I'm not doing enough.
- I can't seem to ever get things right.
- This is all I deserve.
- I'm worthless.
- I hate myself.
- I feel humiliated.
- I'm a failure.
- Maybe I am abusive?

Down the wormhole of fear and self-deception you go. Each one of these lies you tell yourself is an attack against yourself.

Until you learn to like, respect, and trust yourself, you will not believe you deserve to be loved in a romantic relationship. Your self-esteem will remain low and you will look to be loved from the outside. You may be terrified to go within—and explore the thoughts, beliefs, and feelings you hold about yourself. Until now, you have not been ready to do the inner work of building confidence and self-esteem. To do so, requires that you care enough about yourself and your feelings. You have to believe you matter. Until now, you have kept yourself on the back burner of life—putting your mate's feelings and needs before your own.

For the pleaser to begin the process of personal growth, he must acknowledge that creating happiness and love is an inside job. This important work of self-improvement cannot begin, so long as he continues to actively resist working on himself—and pours every ounce of energy into keeping his mate stable, just to prevent another attack.

In his avoidance and abandonment of self, the pleaser holds critical beliefs about the value he adds to his romantic relationship:
- I don't deserve to be loved by my girlfriend or wife.
- I feel inadequate—like something is wrong with me.
- I don't feel good enough. She's so attractive. She's out of my league.
- I won't be able to eat, sleep, or function if this relationship ends.
- I can never get things right.
- If I leave, she's going to take the kids and exploit me financially.
- I am too weak to make it through the fall-out.
- I can't seem to make any of my romantic relationships work. I always screw things up.
- I always get treated so poorly.
- Women always end up finding something wrong with me.
- No one else is going to want me.
- My life will be worse if I leave.
- I'll never find anyone else.
- I'm better off staying where I am and riding it out.

The pleaser is often unaware he ***can*** change his negative beliefs and the mental patterns he holds about himself. Even though he feels inadequate and undesirable, the pleaser is unaware he can develop a more positive self-concept. He is also unaware that happiness and confidence must be created within.

Until you begin to develop a positive mind-set, you will continue to remain your own worst enemy. You must consciously decide—if you are willing to do the work of self-improvement—and accept the responsibility for your own psychological and emotional well-being.

Imagine if you began working on yourself—by turning the mirror around and taking a closer look at your own wants and needs. What if you put the effort into changing your negative beliefs about yourself? Can you imagine making a conscious decision to wake up and inspire yourself with life-affirming beliefs about who you are—and what you are capable of achieving in your life?

Throughout your relationship, you have been attempting to feel lovable by getting your mate to treat you better via pleasing, accommodation, and submission. How is that healthy? Obviously, it is not! It is both allowing yourself to be controlled and attempting to control her— to soothe your interpersonal anxiety caused by your mate's negative feelings and critical words. You can choose to refocus your energy by no longer personalizing the abuse—or caring what your mate thinks about you.

What if you began telling yourself the truth about your abusive relationship, starting with:
- "Her abuse has nothing to do with me."
- "Everything she says about me is a projection about herself."
- "She is often describing how she feels about herself and what she is doing."
- "Clearly, we were never a good fit."
- "I know I ignored a ton of red flags."
- "Only insecure individuals lash out and abuse their partners."

- "I am ready to accept that I'm never going to get through to her—or get her to understand me."
- "I can decide how I respond to her abuse—and what I'm ultimately going to do about it."
- "I will keep reminding myself the abuse has nothing to do with me—and let go of caring what she thinks of me."
- "I'm going to beat her to the punch and stay two steps ahead of her."

You can consciously decide that you are not responsible for the baggage, insecurities, opinions, and poor mental health of your mate. The truth is: the disapproval, rejection, and abuse of another human being has nothing to do with you. It is all about them. You are not responsible for the mistakes, judgements, insults, and anger of another individual.

Have you ever considered that you were manipulated as a young boy to feel responsible for your parent's insecurities, judgments, high expectations, wrong-doings, anger, guilt-inducing communication, and overall lack of personal accountability?

You have likely internalized the blame and manipulation of others in your family—creating deeply ingrained beliefs—that it was you causing the problems in your family. Overtime, you developed a critical self-concept and came to believe it was your fault whenever you were met with rejection or abuse from others.

Are you aware that you have the power to change your negative beliefs about yourself—and let go of caring what others think about you? You can develop a positive mind-set—first by understanding that your mate's abusive behavior has nothing to do with you.

You have probably heard the adage: You must love yourself before you can be in a loving relationship. It turns out, that this is true! Yet, men and women have been attempting to bypass this inconvenient truth since the beginning of time—hoping to hook up, find, and keep a lover—without ever having to like, respect, or trust themselves.

Low self-esteem can only lead to dependency issues and hostile relationships. Often it is only after years of attempting to fix their mate and tolerating abusive treatment, that some individuals seek professional help—or let go of their toxic relationship. Often depressed, anxious, and full of resentment towards their mate for "failing" to love them in a way they wanted or needed to be loved, these individuals lament about how poorly they have been treated—oblivious to the role they have played by not setting or holding boundaries from the get go—or walking away when conditions became toxic.

Had these individuals had any respect for themselves, they would not tolerate toxic behavior—no matter how much love they felt towards their mate. What does it say about an individual's self-esteem if he or she tolerates poor treatment and abuse? What does it say about an individual's self-esteem if he or she attempts to fix, force, or change someone?

I see so many individuals in therapy vilify their partner for treating them "horribly," but see nothing unhealthy about remaining in a toxic, romantic relationship.

The bottom line is this: If an individual is ever to attract and sustain an authentic, loving relationship, he must first develop confidence in himself—to be himself and remain himself—as opposed to turning himself over to his mate—and giving pieces of himself away.

Pleasing never works! Unfortunately, many partners forgo the development of self-awareness and self-esteem needed to create a healthy romantic relationship—hoping to find love—without ever having to heal childhood trauma, learn to trust themselves, develop confidence to know who they are, and remain true to themselves.

Pleasers feel a subjective sense of inadequacy in their romantic relationships—and lack the confidence to express their wants, needs, and feelings. They have not developed the self-esteem needed to set boundaries—and feel a nagging sense of self-consciousness—that drives their deeply-ingrained need to please. Frequently feeling insecure, the pleaser lives in fear of screwing things up, and then feeling responsible for the anger and abuse of his mate.

For both the pleaser and the narcissist, rejection is tantamount to death. Should the relationship end, both will feel as if they "failed" and see it as "proof" of their worthlessness, inadequacy, and undesirability. Hence, the negative beliefs they already hold about themselves will be reinforced.

The truth is, individuals with low self-esteem do not have to endure toxic romantic relationships, nor should they. They are not stuck. Many just stubbornly refuse to accept the relationship is not a good fit—or that they would be better off without their toxic mate in their life. Everyone has the power to heal and build self-esteem. Unfortunately, some resist confronting the enemy within (their control issues and poor self-esteem) as this means letting go, being alone, and working on themselves. They would have to learn to care for themselves—and let go of caring what other people might think of them.

All individuals have the power to change their negative beliefs and stories they tell themselves about their worth in romantic relationships, who they can attract, and how they deserve to be treated.

What if you began reframing your story about rejection and abuse (as it relates to your self-concept)? What if you stopped feeling responsible for the words and feelings of your mate (the judgments, blame, lack of personal accountability, and anger) that she so comfortably projects onto you?

You are not responsible for your mate's caustic perceptions and emotions. By feeling responsible for her feelings, you are unable to develop trust in yourself. Hence, you are more likely to hemorrhage personal power—by giving credibility to your mate's words and feelings about you. How can you possibly feel good about yourself if you let your mate define who you are?

You do not have to go through life with low self-esteem. You do not have to internalize or feel responsible for your mate's abuse. You can begin telling yourself a new story about the abuse you receive from your mate.

Begin by reminding yourself:
- "Her abuse has nothing to do with me."
- "It's all about her own crap—and it always will be."
- "She's never going to change—because she doesn't think she has to."
- "Submission is not going to make her treat me better."
- "Attempting to be perfect will not make her love me more."
- "I cannot change or control her. Pleasing has been my attempt to do just that."
- "I do not have the power to make another love me."
- "I am in charge of my own thoughts, perceptions, feelings, and responses."
- "I am a good man."
- "I am a good father."
- "I am replaying childhood trauma in my abusive relationship."
- "I can recover and develop a positive mind-set if I choose to do the work."
- "I will continue to quietly detach—and continue to reframe rejection and abuse."
- "I'm getting out of this—no matter how hard it is."
- "By no longer trying to save my mate, I will save myself.

- "Now that I'm learning about narcissism, pleasing, and strategies to build self-worth, I can see my escape as an opportunity to heal, grow, and develop confidence in myself."

What if you started to tell yourself the truth about your abusive relationship? And the choices you have in your life? You can continue to shift your negative and erroneous beliefs about yourself—to positive, life-affirming ones:

- I am not responsible for her perceptions, feelings, and behavior.
- The abuse can only affect me—if I believe it.
- We are clearly not a good fit.
- I am powerless to fix or save anyone. When I do this, I abandon myself.
- I can create the life I truly want.
- I am allowing the abuse to continue by staying.
- It is my responsibility to leave—and learn to let go of toxic people in my life.
- I can't heal my abandonment issues if I refuse to let go of toxic people.
- I am not who she says I am.
- I am enough—and I matter—and will eventually find a good partner once I have escaped and done some work on myself.
- I deserve far more than the abuse I'm receiving.
- I will now choose to do this work—of excavating and changing my beliefs—and being kinder to myself.
- By consciously choosing new thoughts and beliefs, I am feeling more confidence and hope about my future.

By catching yourself—should you start to believe your mate's vitriolic words—and reminding yourself the abuse has nothing to do with you, you begin to develop a more positive mindset. Once you excavate your negative beliefs, write them down, and change them to the truth about who you are—you will begin to see yourself accurately and let go of caring what your mate thinks about you.

You have been too hard on yourself—for too long. You no longer have to be your own worst enemy.

Are you ready to change your internal beliefs? Are your ready to begin building yourself up—and deliberately making yourself feel better?

Instead of blaming yourself after an attack, you can choose to tell yourself the truth about who you are, what you have said or done, and what you deserve.

- "I deserve to be treated with respect."
- "I deserve to be trusted."
- "It is my job to learn boundaries—and to hold boundaries. And the only boundary that works in an abusive relationship—is separation."
- "I have done nothing to warrant my mate's abusive words."

By repeating these words to yourself every morning (even if you do not yet believe them), you will begin to release the feelings of guilt, shame, and humiliation you carry. As you make this a daily practice, you will eventually no longer feel responsible for the feelings of others—and continue to differentiate yourself from others' approval.

Since you began reading this book, you have learned a great deal about pleasing and narcissism—and become more conscious of your behavior—and that of your mate's. You are expanding your knowledge, and now becoming increasingly self-aware—as you reclaim your power, one piece at a time.

You are learning that you can consciously decide to change your internal beliefs—and no longer feel responsible for the feelings of others.

You have the power to make different decisions about your worth—by choosing to **consciously** tell yourself:

- "I decide I'm enough."
- "I decide that I deserve to be treated better."
- "I decide to be emotionally confident and secure."
- "I decide that I deserve to be in a healthy romantic relationship—once I have done some healing."
- "I decide to like, respect, and trust myself."
- "I decide to be true to myself—by no longer compromising myself."
- "I decide to print out my new beliefs—and read them first thing in the morning—every day."
- "I decide to no longer blame myself for the disapproval, rejection, or abuse of others."

This is self-awareness. This is consciousness. You have the power to heal your childhood trauma by integrating new beliefs about yourself and let go of feeling responsible for the feelings of others.

Now that you know you are **not** responsible for the feelings and decisions of others, you can begin to trust yourself, and validate your own perceptions, thoughts, beliefs, and feelings. You can also decide to forgive yourself for believing you are worthless, inadequate, and undesirable. Forgiveness is a very powerful form of release.

When children internalize the blame, guilt, and manipulation of authority figures in their lives, they blame themselves for having caused the conflict, disapproval, and rejection of their parents. Children then come to believe they have done something "wrong" or "bad." They interpret their mistakes (as determined by their parents)—to mean they are "worthless," or "stupid"—and come to believe it is they who are responsible for the negative reactions, feelings, and abusive behavior of their parents. Eventually, they decide they are not worthy of love and respect.

This is how traumatized children come to believe they are "flawed," "inadequate," and "unlovable" by the time they reach adulthood. These same internal beliefs remain until they are released. Each time the young man experiences conflict, blame, judgment, or rejection, he automatically blames himself for doing something wrong. Hence, he comes to believe he is causing his own abuse or rejection. Each time a romantic relationship ends, the young man blames himself to be the cause of it—as if he has "failed" as an adequate love partner. He then reinforces his own critical belief system about his worth.

Surely no one who truly liked, trusted, and respected themselves would choose to remain in an abusive relationship—regardless of whether they loved their mate. Abuse is not love.

You can begin to do this inner work of changing your thoughts and beliefs. A daily practice of reading these thoughts and beliefs will provide inspiration and motivation—and assist you in integrating positive beliefs and uplifting messages into your self-concept. In other words, you *can* deliberately decide to make yourself feel better—and release guilt, fear, and shame.

You begin to understand the power of authenticity—of liking, trusting, and respecting yourself—as you begin feeling better about yourself and release worry and the anticipation of negative outcomes.

It is not in any lover's job description to make you feel better about yourself—or feel more lovable. It is your job to define who you are and to make yourself happy. This is your decision—and your job alone. No one can make you feel lovable if you do not like yourself. It is ultimately your responsibility to build happiness, confidence, and value from the inside.

It is your responsibility to be who you are, define who you are, and know the value you add to a romantic relationship—before you enter a romantic relationship. You must have the confidence to be (and remain) your authentic self— aware that it is your uniqueness that attracts someone in the first place. The moment your try to "make" or "get" someone to love you, you begin the process of giving yourself away—one piece at a time.

Many individuals feel a lack of confidence upon entering a romantic relationship—and try to hide their fears and doubts from their mate. Pleasers immediately go about impressing, morphing, and earning their mate's love—by becoming whoever she needs him to be. They will do anything to keep their mate interested and happy—and anything to avoid potential loss, conflict, or rejection.

Approval seeking and dependency issues can certainly be released— using the many strategies I have outlined in this book. But the disease must be healed from the inside as well—by looking within, reflecting, and excavating the negative thoughts and beliefs your hold about yourself. In this way, you come to know and differentiate yourself from others.

You cannot be yourself (authentically)—if you need to be liked by every person in your life. Some are not going to like you—and it has nothing to do with you. It is your job to look inside and decide what you see— and how you feel about yourself. Until now, you have been allowing your narcissistic mate to define your reality since the beginning of your toxic relationship. You have been more concerned about "keeping the peace" and "sweeping things under the carpet," than holding your personal power—and expressing your own perceptions and emotions.

Without developing an intrinsic sense of self-worth and emotional intelligence before entering a romantic relationship, a pleaser feels he must be perfect to be loved by his mate. Always on high alert for judgment, conflict, or rejection, he ignores his own wants, needs, and feelings—hoping to secure the love of his mate.

His internal dialogue sounds something like the following:
- "What if I mess things up?"
- "What if she changes her mind about me?"
- "I don't deserve to be in a good relationship."
- "She's out of my league."
- "What if I offend her?"
- "Why would a really attractive woman be interested in me?"
- "I don't believe I deserve her."
- "I'm too fat."
- "I'm too thin."
- "I'm ugly."
- "I don't deserve to be loved by someone I really want."
- "I don't deserve to be treated any better."

Can you identify with some of these beliefs and critical perceptions? If you have not recovered from your trauma, you will still possess a negative self-concept—in which you simply do not believe you deserve the unconditional love of a partner you are interested in.

You can search your self—and notice your internal records, beliefs, and ways you talk to yourself. You can change your negative mental records, beliefs, and thought patterns—and inspire yourself to develop a positive mindset over time. Begin with any positive thoughts and beliefs I have suggested in this chapter—and add uplifting messages, thoughts, or beliefs that resonate with the *new* you. Begin this practice of changing your self-concept from the inside.

Other positive messages are:
- "I deserve to be treated well in all my relationships."
- "It is my job to teach people how to treat me—and let go of toxic relationships."
- "I will be successful escaping, releasing my need to please, and no longer care whether some do not like me."

- "Ironically, when I release my need for approval, I end up getting the approval of others."
- "I decide who I am."
- "I decide I am enough."
- "I can consciously decide I deserve to receive love."
- "As I consciously choose new thoughts and beliefs about myself and the abuse, new opportunities, ideas, and goals will come to me."
- "I will continue to feel more confident about myself—and trust that everything will work out for the better."

Releasing your tendency to worry and letting go of negative beliefs will take time—but this is how it starts. Your purpose is to inspire yourself, build yourself up, and release old emotions that no longer serve you.

You are responsible for your own mental health—and that of your children's. You are not responsible for the judgments, criticism, and caustic feelings of others. Remember to keep your guard up—and remind yourself that you are no longer buying what your mate is selling. Until you are out of your house, it will be difficult to utilize more overt forms of disengagement—like hanging up the phone, saying NO, walking away, or simply not responding at all. Until then, you can utilize invisible boundaries, and avoid having discussions—or putting yourself in situations where you do not have a quick plan to disengage.

It is difficult to disengage while living together. But as you plan when and how you will escape—you can battle feelings of guilt about how you are "lying" to your mate—by not telling her about your plans. Feel your guilt and know you are doing nothing wrong. You are making the right, responsible decision to get out of an abusive relationship.

When you begin exercising your invisible boundaries, no longer discuss your feelings, act as if nothing is out of the ordinary, and challenge your guilt about not discussing your plans, your narcissistic mate is likely to notice some changes. Reassure her that nothing is out of the ordinary. Time is now of the essence. Do not kick the can down the road.

You can cope with whatever you set your mind to—and whatever problem you encounter in life. Changing your beliefs about who you are—and what you are capable of—is critical to the development of self-esteem. Your narcissistic mate is forcing you to make this critical decision to begin putting yourself first—and to choose which path you will now take at this fork in the road. Growth or decay?

You both attracted each other from a place of unhealed trauma and low self-esteem. Your narcissistic mate is never going to get help and work on herself—so it looks like it is up to you! Are you going to choose **you**—and stop abandoning yourself?

Remember to remind yourself of the following truths:
- "I'm not going to blame myself anymore."
- "It's been me rejecting and abandoning myself."
- "I'm deciding to take my power back—one step at a time."
- "With consciousness, I can make different decisions."
- "There is power in a decision."
- "I was not aware I was abandoning myself—but I am now."
- "I can no longer unsee what I now see."
- "I forgive myself for blaming myself to be causing her instability and angry rhetoric."
- "I am making the conscious decision to trust I will meet a healthy partner in the future."
- "My life will definitely get better once I am out."

Your younger self did not know any better when you met your abusive mate, but now that you do—you can choose differently. Work on changing your negative thoughts and beliefs about yourself as you plan your escape.

Are you feeling better about yourself and more hopeful about your future?

11

Feeling Man

Pleasers have not yet learned to identify, feel, and **process** painful emotions. They live in fear, "what ifs," and anticipation of negative outcomes. Worry is their constant companion. Pleasers often imagine every possible worst-case scenario and fear it may well come true. Hence, they often decide it is better to stay put—right where they are—careful not to make any big decisions—in case they land in a worse position than they currently are. The following are some of the pleaser's negative thought patterns:

- *If I acknowledge how I truly feel, then I'll have to leave.*
- *It is better to stay and have somebody, than to leave and be alone.*
- *What's she going to do if I leave? She might succeed in destroying me. I know she's going to try and steal the kids from me.*
- *What if she turns everyone against me? What if she ruins my reputation?*
- *What if I'm devastated and cannot function anymore? What if I cannot eat, sleep or work—when I leave? I don't feel strong enough.*

- *What if she changes after I leave—and meets someone? What if someone else makes her happy?*
- *What if I change my mind after I leave and want to go back?*
- *What if another guy moves in and starts parenting my kids?*
- *What if I never find anyone else? I'm terrified to be alone.*
- *I'll have to do everything myself. I cannot do it all on my own.*
- *I don't want to start over.*
- *I'll feel guilty for lying to her—and not telling her I'm leaving.*
- *That would be mean and selfish.*
- *I won't be able to afford a new house, child-support, and alimony.*
- *How am I going to stand up for myself—after the fall-out and get shared custody?*
- *After every attack, I feel like giving up.*
- *I don't have the energy to get out.*
- *I'm a failure.*
- *Who is going to want me?*
- *The fall-out is going to feel like being hit by a tsunami.*

So many questions. So many fears—and terrifying "what-if's." In order to avoid the emotional pain of the above thoughts, partners often rationalize the abuse—convincing themselves the relationship is better than it is—or will eventually get better. But deep down, the pleaser often knows he should be leaving, but his negative thoughts (like those above) produce so much fear, he ignores his current reality—and clings to rationalizations that he can stay and make things work.

Rationalizations serve the purpose of repressing painful emotions by avoiding reality. Back and forth, the pleaser goes in his mind—between staying and escaping. When the terror becomes too much, he caves—and rationalizes things will somehow get better. The pleaser thinks to himself:

- *Maybe we can still work things out?*
- *Maybe she will eventually see how hard I'm trying.*
- *I'm hoping she eventually sees what she's doing to me.*

- *My guts are telling me I have to leave.*
- *Deep down, I know what I should be doing.*
- *I have to get out soon.*
- *I'll eventually figure out how I'm coming across in such an offensive manner.*
- *Maybe things aren't as bad as I think they are.*
- *Sometimes she treats me okay.*
- *I'll eventually be able to make her happy.*
- *She's crazy. Why am I sticking around?*
- *I have to lawyer up and face this head on.*
- *I know I can prove myself to her.*
- *I'm staying for the kids.*
- *I'm going to traumatize the children if I leave. But I see how the kids are suffering now.*
- *I can see how things are getting worse—and how the abuse is ramping up.*
- *She's denying she cheated on me and physically assaulted me.*
- *She can convince herself of anything.*
- *I'm not going to find anyone else.*
- *Someone is better than no one.*
- *I'll keep trying to make things work—even though her attacks are crippling me.*
- *She still turns me on. That's nuts.*
- *I know I should be leaving—but I don't feel strong enough.*
- *I'm so humiliated I'm in this mess.*

These conflicting thought patterns—between knowing on a cognitive level that you should be leaving yet rationalizing you can stay—is referred to as cognitive dissonance—a term used in psychology to describe the mental anguish that results from holding two opposing beliefs. In a narcissistic relationship, the pleaser usually fluctuates between what he knows (cognition that he should be leaving), and the reality he fears facing (loss, ongoing abuse, separation, and fall-out).

This state of cognitive dissonance is precisely where the pleaser gets "stuck." Hence, he rationalizes—and lies to himself that the relationship will eventually get better—for the purpose of soothing his painful feelings. While his coping strategy makes the pleaser feel better in the moment, he cannot sustain this comfort—because another attack is just around the corner. Then, when it invariably comes, the cognition (knowing what the debilitating abuse is doing to him and his children) kicks in—and he is back to knowing what he must do.

After an attack, the pleaser knows how crazy his mate is—and how senseless his reality is. He spends incredible amounts of mental energy attempting to figure abusive incidents out—analyzing if he actually did do anything wrong or offensive. Then, after a couple of days, he begins to rationalize he can potentially stay and do better—or his mate will see what she is doing. How can she not, right? Attempting to make himself feel better, the pleaser has minimized his abuse—to calm his terror of letting go and stepping into the unknown. Humiliation, guilt, terror, and feelings of worthlessness are the emotional consequences of trivializing his abuse. In other words, a pleaser is creating his own terror by lying to himself that he can make things work. The lies keep him in his abusive reality.

What if you told yourself the truth:
- "I know my kids are suffering from the chaos and abuse."
- "I'm doing nothing substantial to protect them."
- "I can see a lot more of my abusive reality now."
- "I can muster the courage to get the hell out."
- "I'm terrified to leave, but I now have the knowledge and strategies to do it."
- "Who in their right mind would tolerate this debilitating abuse? I have to get real with myself."
- "I always deceive myself into thinking she's going to stop— and even though I love the idea of that—it is not reality."

If you begin telling yourself the truth, what feelings would you then create? As opposed to avoiding your painful feelings caused by the lies you tell yourself? In your avoidance—and all the rationalizations you use to make yourself feel better—you unwittingly create significantly more mental and emotional anguish in the long-run.

Your abusive relationship is simply the devil you know.

In your choice to avoid the terror of making the crucial, necessary, and responsible decision to escape—you avoid facing your fears and scare yourself back into the same poor coping methods. The truth is—you are **not** caring for yourself, nor are you investing in your psychological and emotional self. You are not prioritizing yourself. In essence, you are using your narcissistic mate as a distraction—to avoid the work of personal growth (of going inside and eradicating the rationalizations and lies you tell yourself).

Women have been talking about their emotions and the concept of self-esteem for ages. Do you not think they are on to something extremely valuable? Many men, on the other hand, have been repressing their emotions—as if they are not real men if they learn to go inside, listen to their intuition, and release negative thoughts and beliefs that no longer serve them.

I am passionate about teaching men how to do this—to become *feeling* men—and to learn the power this process holds. Is it not time that men become more comfortable with their emotions, focus on changing their thought patterns, and release the rationalizations and lies they tell themselves?

So often, men are so afraid to go within and consciously change thinking patterns—because it involves dealing with their feelings and making healthy choices in their lives. That is not a very masculine thing to do, right? Are you kidding? Becoming a feeling man is becoming a real man—a strong man—and an authentically empowered man. Unfortunately, most men have been taught to ignore their feelings— and focus only on the external. By focusing externally on their narcissistic mate, too many men ignore their feelings and rationalize things will somehow get better. In their radical avoidance of emotions, they inadvertently create far more chaos and drama in their lives.

Feeling massive internal conflict (on top of ongoing abuse), your resilience and resolve is significantly impaired. Hence, you steer clear of getting support, hide how bad the situation is from others, and "take it like a man." Moreover, you ignore your own gut feelings and intuition, telling yourself that leaving will result in even more painful feelings. But all you are really doing, is avoiding yourself and dishonoring your emotions. In the end, these poor coping tactics backfire—because you end up trivializing the debilitating psychological and emotional consequences of your own abuse.

While all this torment and chaos is going on inside your mind—you may just give up and accept your lot in life. But in giving up on yourself, you will continue to weaken under the pressure of the abuse. Instead of ripping the band aid off, and just going for it—you end up making the same irrational decision to stay.

Why? Because you are playing out your unhealed childhood trauma— and still attempting to get your mate's approval—while avoiding the hard work of healing, personal growth, and building confidence within yourself. You would rather be poisoned by your narcissistic mate, and continue to internalize the abuse by telling yourself:

- "Maybe I did intend, say, or do what she says I intended, said, or did."
- "Maybe something is seriously wrong with me."
- "Maybe I am coming across in an offensive manner."
- "Maybe I *am* a narcissist. She keeps telling me I am."
- "I don't deserve to have anyone healthy and kind."

- "I'm a failure in relationships."
- "I've always been desperate to be loved—when it comes to a love partner."
- "I can't seem to get anyone to love me."
- "I feel inadequate. Flawed. Useless. And worthless."

This is how pleasers talk to themselves. In reality, pleasers are abusing themselves—frequently critical and self-loathing:

- "I don't deserve to be loved."
- "I'm not going to get anyone else."
- "I can't stand the idea of her sleeping with someone else."
- "I'll never see my kids."

Then back to dissonance:

- "I'll eventually convince her I'm not trying to harm her."
- "I'll succeed in getting her to love me—and to treat me better."
- "I know I can earn her love—and prove myself to her."
- "Even if I can't, there's no way I'm leaving."
- "I consider myself a loyal family man."

The pleaser often attempts to convince himself—by lying to himself—that he is making the right decision to stay, when he is clearly not. "I'm staying for the kids," is just words. It sounds so virtuous, does it not? In reality, the pleaser is just telling himself another lie—to avoid the pain of what he knows he must do. He just refuses to admit the truth to himself—that the children's mental health is deteriorating before his eyes. He knows he is modelling a bad relationship—yet he keeps hiding this truth from himself and others. Ironically, the pleaser often thinks other people cannot see his abusive relationship—when the truth is, many that know him—do.

Despite their dysfunctional reality, pleasers rarely walk into my office and say, "I'd really like to change my mindset and challenge my negative beliefs. I know I need to work up the courage to leave. Can you help me do this?"

Instead, many are consumed with thoughts of self-loathing and cognitive dissonance—not interested in escaping their abusive reality. Pleasers need to confront their cognitive dissonance and the lies they tell themselves—and admit they have a tendency towards self-deception.

By distracting themselves via pleasing, abused men avoid facing the truth of what is really happening inside their abusive relationship. They avoid the work of going inside and challenging their negative beliefs and fears—preferring to live in self-doubt and abuse as opposed to facing the terror of leaving—and an unknown future. Many would rather I confirm the abusive relationship can be fixed, than work on themselves—by facing their abandonment issues and learning to stand up for themselves. The latter requires they get honest with themselves and honor what they know to be true—to ultimately learn to be feeling men. These are the first steps of personal growth (of investing in yourself).

You must decide to step out of your comfort zone—and make the courageous decision to invest in yourself—by undergoing the legitimate suffering of change, grief, and letting go. This is probably exactly where you are. Hence, it is essential to address your cognitive dissonance, listen to your truth deep down, and release the lies you keep telling yourself.

When cognitive dissonance is addressed, real hope and optimism can be developed. In turn, self-awareness is built—and an intrinsic sense of self-worth, trust, and belief in yourself. Indecisiveness is replaced with the ability to trust yourself and make wiser decisions. Once you begin to reduce cognitive dissonance, you become increasingly capable of releasing more judgments and negative beliefs you hold about yourself and about what you deserve.

In their desperate quest for external approval, validation, and love—the narcissist and pleaser simply do not know who they are. In seeking to have their empty spaces filled by the other, each ignore their own feelings—and make no real effort to pay attention to themselves. As such, both cannot develop emotional awareness, internal strength, or develop a strong identity inside the abusive relationship.

Living with this low self-esteem is not a recommended strategy for successful living. What if, instead, you reframed your abuse and began telling yourself the truth:

- "The abuse has nothing to do with me."
- "It is all about her mental illness and childhood trauma."
- "I can consciously decide who I am, how I feel, and what I deserve."
- "I'm no longer giving away my personal power."
- "She has no right to decide how I feel, who I am, or how I act."
- "These are my rights."
- "I can use her as a catalyst to learn how to stand up for myself and begin to develop self-esteem."
- "She is literally forcing me to invest in myself, develop skills to improve my self-esteem, and escape this hostage taking."
- "In reality, she's pushing me to like, trust, and respect myself."
- "Without her, I may not have become aware of my disease to please."
- "Ultimately, she's forcing me to let go of my need to control—and begin working on myself."
- "I don't want to keep caring about what other people think of me."
- "I decide who I am."
- "I can consciously decide the abuse has nothing to do with me."
- "Her failure to see who I am—is nothing but a reflection of herself."

- "Her abusive attacks are simply projections of herself."
- "She has no idea who she is."
- "Had it not been for her, I may well have stayed a door mat for the rest of my life."

Can you feel the *truth* about the above statements? About what they mean—as they pertain to your self-worth? About your intrinsic value in a love relationship?

The truth is, you attracted your mate into your life experience to teach you some important lessons—and you are teaching her some important lessons as well. She is teaching you to stop being a door mat, learn who you are, reclaim your personal power, and become the man you are meant to be.

Your mate is teaching you to put yourself first (into the driver's seat of your life)—as opposed to viewing yourself as some kind of after-thought who has no right to his own voice? Imagine if you practice and apply the knowledge and strategies you have learned in this book ... right now? Imagine what life may look like in two months from now? Or two years from now?

What will your life look like once you are out? What will happiness look like? What will it feel like to have your freedom, dignity, and self-respect? To heal your childhood trauma and fully release your need to please? To trust yourself and learn to love yourself?

What if you reversed the energy you put into pleasing—and invested that precious energy into you—by first reframing the abuse from "It is always me," to "It Has Nothing to do with Me." In reality, you are doing nothing to cause each abusive episode, with the exception of choosing to stick around and take it—thereby making yourself a human punching bag. In the end, you are responsible to yourself and your children. There is simply no good rationalization or justification for tolerating abuse.

Honesty with self—is the key to unlocking and tapping into your potential—and recognizing what you truly deserve. I often hear the ego talking in clients:

- "I don't want to have to leave."
- "I hope I can make the relationship work."
- "I cannot afford to leave."
- "I'm staying for the kids."
- "Maybe she'll eventually see how poorly she's treating me—and stop once she understands how I'm feeling?"

Instead, would it not be healthier to admit the truth to yourself?

- "My partner is a narcissist."
- "Narcissists usually do not heal."
- "I am being abused."
- "Narcissistic abuse does (without exception) get worse over time."
- "Am I really comfortable in this hell? Or is it damaging my mental health?
- "Is it really going to be worse when I leave? Or is this just fear talking?

What if you admitted these truths to yourself? Would that not begin to reduce your dissonance by confronting painful feelings and fears—and helping you arrive at the right decision, build confidence, self-awareness, and self-worth. You can succeed in escaping with honesty and confidence in hand. You can make it out—once you confront the enemy within—and the lies you have internalized and continue to tell yourself.

Many years ago, one of my clients accurately stated, "Living with emotional abuse is, by definition, insanity." The reality is—pleasers can be highly irrational, just like their narcissistic counterparts—because they have not healed from childhood trauma. Hence, they continue to process like the small wounded child—who was frequently guilted, manipulated, or not permitted to share his feelings. Healing involves reprograming yourself towards the truth—and shedding the many lies you tell yourself about who you are and what you are worth.

It is time right now—to begin focusing on the truth of your relationship and releasing the lies you keep telling yourself about your current abusive reality. You must be willing to learn the truth about who you are and what you deserve. Of course, there will be strong compulsions at times to hold onto the hope your mate will become healthier. A part of you probably still loves her—even though it is a toxic kind of love. But in this case, even the love you may have is not a reason to hang on and fight for your relationship.

It is up to you to let go of a woman *who* is not who you once thought she was—or hoped she would become. The truth is, your narcissistic mate is just the right person to force you to learn to be true to yourself—and to begin developing a relationship with yourself. Ironically, in the end, it may very well be your narcissistic mate who teaches you that you cannot make another person love you and pushes you to reclaim your personal power.

12

Shifting Hope

When I counsel men who are currently in, or just out of, an abusive relationship, I am often informed later on in a session—that they have experienced what some have called "holy s**t" moments—which are moments of clarity, where an individual arrives at a truth after they have reflected on some of the dynamics we discussed in the previous session.

Some informed me they were initially mad about some of the dynamics I discussed:

- "I was kind of mad at first thinking—how could you know me that well?"
- "How would you know my abusive relationship that well?"
- "And then I realized—you were right about everything you said—and then I went "holy s**t, everything he said was true.""

You may have had a few of these maddening, "holy s**t" moments yourself as you read this book. If so, this is a good sign. It means you see yourself in this book—and the "holy s**t" moments are actually moments of insight and healing. You have already begun your journey.

I have attempted to emphasize throughout the book that self-awareness and self-esteem—can and should be developed throughout the course of life—for the purpose of building a strong sense of self, including the ability to trust yourself. Developing this subjective sense of inner value and respect for yourself involves the powerful ability to discern what you are—and what you are not—responsible for within your interpersonal relationships.

Neither the narcissist—nor the pleaser—trust themselves. Both have developed little ability to take responsibility for their own crap. The mantras of the narcissist are:
- "It is all your fault that I feel this way."
- "I don't trust myself—and desperately need your agreement/ validation at all times."

Narcissists cannot understand why you would want to stay who you are—and why you would not want to change who you are. And then when you choose not to accept their criticism with appreciation and gratitude they feel insulted—as if (in their ass-backwards world) you have criticized **them**.

The mantras of a pleaser are:
- "I feel sorry for you—and will always give you the benefit of the doubt."
- "I'm just living off hope that you will change and respect me."

As you can see, both are hoping to change each other—and both cannot understand why the other is not willing to change themselves.

Both the narcissist and the pleaser have no self-esteem in romantic relationships. Pleasers have not learned to set—or hold personal boundaries—which ultimately include the necessary boundary of separation. And narcissists, on the other hand, could care less about the boundaries of others. Hence, the never-ending trauma bond.

Should the pleaser attempt to set a boundary after being hurt—and take some space, he is usually bombarded with texts full of accusations for behaviors that are not his fault. Ironically, the pleaser begins to feel sorry for his narcissistic mate, begins doubting himself, and re-engages—often apologizing for what he was accused of doing.

He had attempted to step away and take some space for himself—but had then been accused of "running away from his problems." The accusation instills doubt—that perhaps he is "avoiding the issues" or "stone-walling"—when he has simply attempted to set a boundary and take care of himself.

A major problem for the pleaser is the extreme difficulty recognizing the different forms of manipulation coming his way. Hence, he doubts himself and gets guilted back into re-engaging. This is obviously understandable. What is not so clear is the pleaser's other big issue; that he invariably ends up feeling sorry for his abusive mate after he has been manipulated. The latter is a symptom of his own low self-esteem. Between feeling sorry for his mate—and feeling guilty that he may somehow have harmed her, the pleaser makes the same mistake over and over again. Not reflecting on specifically why he experiences so much guilt, he feels sorry for his mate—and feels responsible for her negative feelings towards him.

Certainly, a crucial step towards the development of self-esteem involves self-reflection and personal ownership—including the responsibility of protecting one's feelings by setting and holding boundaries, such as the following:

- "I felt hurt when you said I was running away, when I was actually trying to get away from your aggression."
- "I needed some space—without harassing accusations I was the one avoiding conflict."
- "This is my boundary—and from now on when I tell you to stop—or I need space—then respect that."
- "I am actually trying to self-reflect."
- "This is *the* conversation I am wanting to have—and this is my boundary moving forward. Do you plan on respecting it?"

Pleasers do not have this level of self-esteem. They may attempt to set a boundary, but when the boundary is invariably crossed by their narcissistic mate, they always allow the violation—unaware they are actually responsible for holding a boundary. Should the new, clarified boundary be crossed again, that is a clear indication he is not being respected—nor is he respecting himself (if he is not holding his own boundary).

And now comes another "holy s**t" moment. The only boundary a narcissist will ever respect—is the boundary of a full-on separation. Often pleasers refuse to acknowledge this truth—despite the fact that they experience the truth of what I am saying every day.

To accept this reality, the pleaser would have to accept he cannot fix or save his abusive relationship. For the pleaser, his abandonment issues and the very thoughts of separation put him into a world of perceived, unknown suffering—for which he will often avoid at all costs.

Releasing this fear involves making the terrifying choice—to step into the painful, dark abyss—to resolve trauma, learn to experience and overcome pain for the purpose of developing inner strength and increased self-esteem. This is letting go.

For this to happen, the pleaser must acknowledge that the massive manipulation he is experiencing—and his frail attempts to set and hold boundaries make him an easy target. He must ultimately learn to set and hold boundaries. To accomplish this additional level of self-esteem, he must learn to stand up to his mate, disengage, and address the obvious pattern of manipulation and boundary violations.

Of course, this requires that the pleaser battle his own insecurities—and own guilt he carries from childhood trauma. Guilt is the emotion the pleaser does not want to own. Then, forever blaming his narcissistic mate for "sucking him in," he deflects ownership by voluntarily re-engaging with his abusive mate. Again, the pleaser avoids the personal responsibility of protecting himself—by respecting himself enough to end the relationship. He invariably caves and gives his abusive mate the benefit of the doubt, feels sorry for her, and re-engages yet again.

This is precisely where the pleaser drops the ball. He will invariably allow his narcissistic mate access to him. In this way, he forfeits his responsibility to protect and respect himself. Certainly he cannot overcome his deep feelings of guilt and shame if he cannot resist his impulse to knowingly stepping back in—without acknowledging any type of plan should his manipulative mate cross his boundaries again.

A healthy individual knows that he is ultimately responsible for his own feelings—and for teaching other's how to treat him. He is not about to have anyone disrespect him by violating his boundaries—and demonstrating zero respect for his feelings, wants, and needs. He has already learned boundaries by detaching from toxic individuals in his life.

The narcissist will not respect her partner's boundaries—and the pleaser will not hold his boundaries (if he attempts to set boundaries at all). By not holding his boundaries, he gives his power away and does nothing to protect himself.

The pleaser lives in the eternal hope the narcissist will change—and the narcissist needs the pleaser to change. Their hope is nothing short of denial—the denial of a reality that is so obviously toxic and abusive—as both desperately try to change the other. The narcissist tries to change the pleaser from a horrible human being to a good human being—and the pleaser actively engages in the same dynamic.

Always giving the narcissist the benefit of the doubt—and unable to recognize he is being manipulated (and also manipulating his mate), the pleaser re-engages out of guilt, shame, and feeling sorry for his mate—hoping to help her overcome her many—and avoid facing his own abandonment issues.

As a therapist—the most difficult dynamic to confront when working with pleasers—are their deep, ingrained feelings of guilt, fear of abandonment, and shame—as they cling to the hope they can help or save their mate. Then, in turn, she will eventually return his love.

"I'm not a quitter" and "I don't like to fail" are further mantras of the pleaser that are once again designed to sound like virtues. The real shift the pleaser is required to make—if he is to develop much needed self-esteem is to make the conscious choice to let go—and get to the painful "sweet-spot" of acceptance—that there is nothing he can do to save or change his mate—or to get her to treat him better.

Despite the most ghastly of treatment—the pleaser refuses to learn what is staring him in the face—that his feelings and needs mean nothing to his narcissistic mate. How can the pleaser ever think he can get the love he needs, when his mate is so obviously hateful and vengeful?

When he is faced with the truth that his abusive relationship cannot be fixed, salvaged, or saved, the pleaser often responds with one of his many "Yes buts."

- "Yes, but I'm staying for the children."
- "Yes, but I don't want to share my children."
- "Yes, but I'm worried how she will treat the kids when I'm not around."
- "Yes, but I'm afraid of what she's going to do if I leave."
- "Yes, but I'm worried she'll turn everyone against me."
- "Yes, but I'm afraid of what everyone else will think."
- "Yes, but I'm not a quitter and I don't like to fail."
- "Yes, but I don't like conflict."
- "Yes, but I cannot afford a divorce."

All of these "Yes buts" involve losses—and all are rationalizations and excuses designed to avoid making the necessary choice to protect your psychological and emotional well-being—and that of your children's. At the root of all of these "Yes buts"—are feelings of terror, guilt, shame, and low self-worth. Individuals with low self-worth often feel guilty and worry about worse-case scenarios—of what could happen (as opposed to trusting things will work out and look for the lesson in their experience). Instead, excuses are used to pacify their ego and avoid confronting the pain required to face a fear—for the purpose of resolving the problem at hand.

Your "Yes but" reality is simply not your true reality. It is you looking at your problem of being "stuck" (and facing separation)—by imagining every worst-case scenario you can think of, then believing those scenarios will become your reality. If you believe the choice to escape will result in your imagined fear coming true, you become "stuck" in the doubt, guilt, shame, and self-loathing of your abusive reality. These emotions intensify the longer they are avoided—and the longer you choose to stay.

The root issue in your abusive relationship is that you do not like, trust, or respect yourself. Hence, you place all of your hope on getting your mate to do this job for you. A romantic relationship is not—and will never be—the cure for low self-esteem. Because the pleaser and narcissist have no self-respect and trust in themselves, both freeze at the thought of ending the relationship—and then revert back to denial—to avoid experiencing the pain of letting go.

You are likely to feel a deep sense of guilt and shame for staying and putting up with your abuse, hence you repress your shame by denying reality and imagining some illusionary future—in which you reconnect and win over your mate. As a pleaser, you can be sure you are holding onto some sort of "magical" hope.

What is your hope? Do you really think it could happen? Are you being honest with yourself about what your hope is? Does your hope rest in your mate changing?

The hope that pleasers cling to—even though their narcissistic mate's abuse is escalating in frequency and intensity—is not **genuine** hope. But pleasers use this hope to deny their abusive reality. It is essentially a defense mechanism to avoid the emotional pain that results from the acceptance they are powerless to fix their relationship—and must choose the legitimate pain of letting go. Because the fear of letting go is so great, they become very adept at self-deception and convincing themselves they are "stuck."

When you learn to sit in your own painful feelings—and ask yourself why you feel the way that you do, you will arrive at honest answers within yourself. This is one of the ways insight and emotional intelligence is developed. As you ask yourself what the healthy, responsible decision is moving forward, you will arrive at the answer if you are willing to pay attention—and be true to yourself. If so, you can now take yourself out of denial—by feeling the pain of your truth—and move into the intuitive knowing of what you must do. This honest decision with yourself will provide relief—if you pay attention.

The acceptance that results from sitting in the "sweet spot" of being honest with yourself is a very powerful place to live. From this place of truth, you can navigate through your life and make course corrections from a place of deep feeling—no longer wishing to avoid the necessary and legitimate pain of personal growth. At this point, there is no more feeling stuck in feelings of indecisiveness, guilt, self-doubt, and confusion. As simple as it sounds, this is a very liberating process—as you guide yourself forward from a place of honesty and integrity within yourself. The unknown pain of being true to yourself—will invariably take you into a new comfort zone—and a desire to live from a place of peace, trust, integrity, patience, confidence, and self-respect

Would this decision to value yourself in this way not be worth all of that?

Conclusion

As Carl Yung so eloquently stated: *I am not what happened to me. I am what I choose to become.*

This has been the whole concept behind the book—to ultimately inspire you to heal from your trauma, decide what you deserve, and choose who you become.

This book is ultimately about exercising the courage and honesty to begin the initially painful process of personal growth—by using the pain you are currently in—to force you into the painful sweet spot of acceptance and decisiveness—of letting go and finally releasing your toxic attachment, need to please, self-deception, and self-blame.

In order to undo years of internalized manipulation from the woman you love, you must practice the art of reprograming yourself—and releasing the negative beliefs you carry about yourself—including your tendency towards self-blame.

You have probably been conditioned to feel you needed to be perfect—to be loved. This is not true. How many decades have you held such a painful and unattainable belief system—only to now arrive at the sweet spot of acceptance—and know from the depths of your soul that you truly deserve more.

In the pain and anxiety of your decision—the seeds are planted—as you become *ready* to begin the journey of caring for yourself—and letting go of your need to be seen, heard, and acknowledged by your narcissistic mate. In this bitter-sweet pain, you are at a precipice—of trusting you will no longer tolerate abuse—and trusting you deserve to be treated better! In your pain—comes the emotional acceptance that you cannot change anyone but yourself—and acknowledge you must create love and happiness from within.

It is fascinating how much pain it takes—for those of us who finally (in all our stubborn resistance) turn the mirror around—and choose to become more? To finally take our first steps out of ego—and the need to control others?

As a therapist for many years, I can honestly say that it is painful—and ultimately rewarding (at the same time)—to be a part of an individual's journey—from a place of powerlessness—to a place of healing and personal transformation. Of how long we all prolong this journey of powerlessness—by fighting for love from those who would seek to control or do us harm—before we finally decide we deserve better, learn how to let go—and accept we must build love from within.

Our bonds and attachments to those we love are so powerful—even when we know we are treated poorly, yet for some strange reason—we keep trying, trying, and trying. To seek love is a perfectly natural process—but for those who are traumatized—love is often sought from those who do not love themselves—and therefore have no love to give.

The temptations of habit, self-deception, trauma, low self-esteem, and rejection of ourselves—coalesce at such a huge cost to ourselves. It is so easy to blame others—and often easier to blame ourselves.

The desire to heal—and grow—is not something that comes naturally for most, if any. It seems that significant pain is the motivator—that ultimately forces us to make decisions that we would not otherwise make. If things were just a little better than they were, we might have stayed where we once were. It seems we, as human beings, require so much pain—before we make such a sacred decision to let go, heal, and grow. Until such time we arrive at this sacred moment of truth, we are likely to tolerate deplorable conditions—and resist changing those conditions—because of some egoic hope that we can help another change—even as we avoid the difficult work of changing ourselves.

In all of our hope, we hide from ourselves, keep our eyes closed, and ignore ourselves—even as our self-worth and relationships become more hostile, more dependent, more hate-filled, and more entrenched. Until such time that the pain becomes beyond what we can endure, we will still hope that factors outside of ourselves might change—so that somehow, we will not have to.

In the myriad of defensive and deceptive ways our ego seems to play, we would rather adapt to an ever-worsening reality—than choose an unknown one. It would seem that the pain of initially learning to let go (for all of us)—is both terrifying and excruciatingly painful. In other words, we would rather enslave ourselves to our ultimate, known fears—than choose another path—and step out of our "comfort zone"—because of the anticipated and unknown pain of a new choice.

It seems we would ultimately rather hand our hope to another—who has no desire to look at themself—than turn the mirror around—and look at ourselves to create our own hope-filled future. How terrifying this process of self-reflection is when we have little regard for ourselves.

In my work with individuals, I see so much trauma and self-inflicted suffering that comes from an individual's tendency to criticize themselves. Many do not feel they even deserve to make a mistake—without feeling like an abject failure. Living in their private hell—in a tormented mind so full of self-deception and lies others have told them about themselves—they hide in shame—too humiliated to reveal themselves—because of who they fear they are.

Most that come from trauma—live in their own tormented mind—in states of co-dependency, guilt, shame, unlovability, and fear—all symptoms of low self-esteem. Having not grown up with emotionally-available parents, they were unable to have (or express) their own emotions—and could not experience the validation of being seen, heard, and understood. Under such repressed circumstances, they could not come to see and trust themselves. They were too afraid to look within—to perhaps see what they were manipulated to believe about themselves.

Now as adults, it is not as though their internal fears of self have subsided. Hence, they innately believe that their only chance at love lies in finding another who might somehow, some way love them—as impossible as that might sound to them—if they can but only be perfect enough. To summon the courage to look at themselves for precisely who they think they are—is too terrifying for many. It seems more comfortable to keep these things (emotions, thought patterns, worries, and beliefs) hidden and repressed—than expose themselves to such perceived "ugliness.'

It seems the fear of self-reflection—the act of looking at ourselves—seems too horrifying and fundamentally unattractive for some. But for those who possess the deep need to grow (and acknowledge this internal need to become more), this decision comes at the very moment they hit the sweet spot of acceptance.

This is precisely where the sacred journey of personal growth begins. This involves going within and exploring our inner self—of finally feeling at the depths of our soul that we deserve more—as we pull every ounce of determination, courage, inspiration, and will to say "enough," "I deserve better" and will do whatever it takes to save ourself from the worsening pain we are in. Finally, we learn that we have the power to change those aspects of ourselves or our lives that we would choose to change thus choosing to become more.

It is my sincere hope that the knowledge, awareness, strategies—and ultimately growth—you have developed by reading this book—has motivated you towards becoming more—towards the creation of a far more inspiring life for you and your children. Hopefully, you have been inspired and validated—that what you have endured as a man—is not normal—or okay—or deserved on any level.

By recognizing control and manipulation—in all its various forms— you now have far more insight to see what you are, and are not responsible for—and have the self-esteem to finally release your compulsion to explain and prove yourself—having hopefully entered the sweet spot of acceptance. This sweet spot is the turning point from releasing your need to please—to looking within, building confidence and trust in yourself.

These are extremely powerful steps towards the development of emotional awareness, internal strength, and self-esteem—as you begin releasing your need to be seen, heard and understood by someone who has not begun to turn her lens around—and remains terrified to do so. This is the process out of ego and into vulnerability—a simultaneously terrifying and deeply fulfilling process of self-discovery and opening your heart.

Yet, this is precisely the *courage* you are now exercising—and precisely the journey you are making—into vulnerability and openness—as you no longer feel the same need to hide yourself—trusting you have nothing you need to hide. As you begin looking at yourself, you begin to enjoy putting energy into the development of yourself and your life—and at the same time—feel more inspiration, motivation, determination, self-respect, trust, and real hope.

As you choose to experience the legitimate pain of letting go, with the sole (soul) purpose of freeing yourself from the chains in which you have lived, you begin to like, trust, and respect what you see. No longer do you require approval from the outside—of family, society, religion, or any other external entity. You now begin to acknowledge yourself—and the brilliance of who you are. You now embrace the power of independent thinking.

As you now learn how to validate and trust your own perceptions, emotions, ideas, opinions, beliefs, and decisions, you can clearly see the severe mental health issues of your mate—and trust she has no desire to change. No longer do you need to feel sorry for her—and second guess yourself—as you now understand just how difficult this process of letting go and reversing the mirror has been to undertake.

And so it has been for all of us who have exercised the courage and integrity to make the journey towards authentic power. And here at this sweet spot of acceptance, can we finally see ourselves—and begin to exercise compassion and empathy for the extreme suffering of the human condition.

You are now in the beautiful process of becoming open and honest with yourself by releasing the so-called security (along with the self-deception) of rationalization, excuses, cognitive dissonance, and "Yes buts"—and no longer lying to yourself about a humiliating reality that you are now exercising the courage to release.

Lie after lie is released—as you choose to let go and release yourself from the chains of denial.

Should you have made the decision to escape, can you now feel the relief that comes from being honest with yourself and feel proud of doing what you have put off for so long?

No longer are you choosing to live in a deceptive reality where your sole focus is: "If I can get her the help she needs, I won't have to choose the pain of leaving."

As you work through this letting go process, you will notice the release of self-deception feels relieving—as you now practice prioritizing your own thoughts, feelings, perceptions, and decisions, by remaining true to yourself. By going inside and reflecting on what *you* see—and what *you* experience in any abusive situation (as opposed to internalizing what you are manipulated to believe has happened), and step away from needing to be seen or understood, you begin a powerful process of independent thinking and the ability to trust yourself.

While the sweet spot is still painful and often fraught with anxiety, you can take solace in trusting you are right where you need to be. This pain—and the transition of release towards refection, cannot be avoided in the development of self-esteem and the pursuit of happiness—because in all of your pain, you are making a significant internal shift. You are being honest with yourself—and this development of integrity—is going to launch you light years beyond any pursuit of external approval. This is a *big and powerful* first!

While there is pain and anxiety in this process of letting go, releasing your need to please, and worrying about an unknown future, you can rest assured you are absolutely doing the right thing. Along with practicing your new beliefs, be sure to counter worry and mistrust of your future with visualizing where you wish to be in two months from now—and what your life will look like when you have reclaimed your power—in addition to providing a safe, loving environment for your children to develop and be free to be themselves.

Be willing to sit, and experience any depressive, frightening, and painful emotions including loneliness, jealousy, and even the anger of knowing she will try and exploit you financially—all of it—and any feelings of brutal injustice. Trust these feelings will pass—and trust that you are strong enough to deal with anything, and all will work out better than you imagined—as you exercise the immense courage to take the road less travelled—into a much better place internally and externally—a place of peace, emotional safety, happiness, trust, and freedom.

Self-awareness, self-esteem, and inner-strength are developed when courage is exercised to end toxic or otherwise abusive relationships. Many will not exercise the courage to do this—at their own expense. You, on the other hand, are now saying to yourself: "I deserve better than how I am being treated" … "I am not a victim. I am choosing to do something about my abuse, to get out, and to be happy."

When you think about it, the reality is actually quite simple: If people don't like you, they don't like you. This is not a reflection of you—it is a reflection of them. So long as you own your faults and learn from your mistakes, what more can you do? In learning to release your need to please—and let go of your mate—you are letting go of the need to be liked by those that would seek to harm you—and ultimately every one of your insecurities that result from your need to please—including feeling sorry for people, and giving them the unearned benefit of the doubt.

If some don't like you, they don't like you. So what?

We all have to learn to let go—or forever be chained in pleasing and submission for the remainder of our days. Letting go—involves grieving—not giving in—and **willing** ourselves to persevere through the grief, feelings of jealousy and loss. You just power through it, trust yourself, and persevere to the other side.

But before we end, it is not simply letting go—that pleasers have an aversion to. More specifically, it is their tendency to blame themselves for the relationship failing. This is their deep issue. Pleasers invariably blame themselves for the anger and manipulation of others—as they struggle to *see* they are being punished and controlled. It is this abandonment and blame of self that causes so much of the pleaser's pain of rejection—because he has not been taught any better ways of coping.

> **The pleaser has been manipulated for so long to be the cause of other people's anger—he fully believes it.**

The pleaser avoids abandonment primarily because he blames and abandons himself for causing his own rejection or abuse—whether it be love partners, friends, or family members. It is the pleaser's blame of self that causes the majority of his rejection and abandonment issues— which is why I am helping you to change your beliefs around rejection and abuse. Remember to tell yourself:

- "I am not responsible for the anger of another person."
- "I am not responsible for the decisions of others."
- "I am extremely courageous to be sitting in the sweet spot of acceptance."

This seems to be the biggest battle for the pleaser—in that he blames himself for causing conflict and does not trust himself (on an emotional level) that his partner's hate and anger is not somehow his fault.

Know that just getting away—and getting free from the abuse—will help you release self-blame and negative beliefs. You must learn that you are not responsible for making others happy and doing what they want you to do, nor are you responsible for making them angry if you choose not to comply. This is essentially your trauma—and emotional belief system of guilt and self-blame.

Have you ever really considered why you tolerate the blame heaped your way over the years? Because it is consistent with the internal blame and guilt you emotionally put on yourself.

Releasing self-blame and feelings of guilt, like releasing your need to please, depends on you frustrating the emotion by not acting on it. You may still blame yourself, or feel guilt, when you say, "No," but you just sit with the feelings—knowing they will eventually fade when you remain true to yourself. Building self-esteem requires releasing toxic relationships from your life.

As you learn to be true to yourself, you continue the slow journey out of ego—and into your heart (self-awareness, self-respect, decisiveness, trust, and letting go)—by listening to your emotions and excavating the self-critical beliefs you carry about conflict and rejection.

As you let go of control—in this case the hope (denial) that "love will find a way"—you are learning to like, respect, and trust yourself by processing your emotions on your own (and even better—with a therapist)—and look to release your fears and your tendency to blame yourself. Instead, you instead look for the good (or the lesson) in each experience.

Your mental health, happiness, self-worth, sense of lovability, and boundaries—are ultimately your responsibility to create—and to define—by teaching people how to treat you and to stop accepting responsibility for crap that is not yours to take. This level of self-esteem is only developed when you set and hold boundaries—and work through your tendency to blame yourself for other people's stuff.

Self-awareness, self-worth, self-love, and inner strength come from within—from a sense of knowing who you are—and developing meaning and purpose in your life—by creating the best possible outcomes for you and your children. These attributes cannot be developed by chasing the approval of others.

Until you reach this level of self-esteem—after you hit the sweet spot of acceptance (this inner knowing you deserve to be treated better) and decide you are enough as you are—you no longer make decisions from a place of fear, guilt, and self-blame. You begin to release feelings of guilt as you move forward—no longer feeling responsible for the words and decisions of others. Instead, you exercise the courage and the power to create a wonderful life—no longer settling for the well-worn path of dependency, control, and anger—which ironically in the end, require far more emotional energy than the more rewarding path of personal growth.

I hope you see the irony here. The energy and pain expended and experienced over a lifetime of dependency and decay—is far greater than the energy and pain required to let go of self-blame, grow, and meet your potential.

Assuming you are ready to take full advantage of the knowledge, skills, and strategies in this book, (and choose to put it all into practice), then you are about to embark upon an amazing journey of self-discovery—and the creation of an amazing life of trusting yourself, integrity, purpose, and authentic power. It is my sincere hope that you decide to make this inspiring, fulfilling, and rewarding journey. You are most definitely worth it!

About The Author

Jim Butler has served as a licensed, registered counsellor in Saskatoon for over seventeen years. His emphasis is on individual and couple counselling. In those seventeen years, Jim has become a trusted authority on emotional abuse and personal growth/transformation.

Jim has helped hundreds of people find the clarity, strength, and inspiration to overcome challenges in their lives. He has authored articles on emotional abuse. His book, *Releasing Your Need to Please,* focused on the growing phenomenon of female emotional abuse towards male partners. This book is written for both sexes and in no way minimizes the emotional abuse men inflict on women.

Jim has helped many people (both men and women) to recognize what emotional abuse is and how to empower themselves to resolve it. He is committed to providing a safe, non-judgmental atmosphere for his clients.

To find out more about Jim and his practice, see www.acacounselling.ca